THE STATESMEN

THE STATESMEN

The Parallel Lives of
Phocion of Athens and Cato the Younger of Rome

AS TOLD BY PLUTARCH

Translated by C. Scot Hicks & David V. Hicks

CiRCE
Concord, NC

Published in the USA by the CiRCE Institute
© 2021 by C. Scot Hicks and David V. Hicks

ISBN: 978-1-7347853-3-3

For information:
CiRCE Institute
81 McCachern Blvd.
Concord, NC 28025
info@circeinstitute.com
www.circeinstitute.com

Cover design by Graeme Pitman
Layout by Courtney Sanford

The CiRCE Institute is a non-profit 501(c)3 organization that exists to promote and support classical education in the school and in the home. We seek to identify the ancient principles of learning, to communicate them enthusiastically, and to apply them vigorously in today's learning settings through curriculum development, teacher training, leadership development events, online training, and a content-laden website.

To learn more please visit circeinstitute.org.

Using history as a mirror, I try by whatever means I can to improve my own life and to model it by the standard of all that is best in those whose lives I write. As a result, I feel as though I were conversing and indeed living with them; by means of history, I receive each one of them in turn, welcome and entertain them as guests and consider their stature and their qualities and select from their actions the most authoritative and the best with a view to getting to know them. What greater pleasure could one enjoy than this or what more efficacious in improving one's own character?

—Plutarch, *Life of Timoleon*

CONTENTS

Introduction.. 1

The Life of Phocion of Athens.. 10

The Life of Cato the Younger.. 70

Appendices.. 183

Bibliography.. 193

INTRODUCTION

I

To strike thee dumb, turn up thy eyes to Cato!

There may'st thou see to what a godlike height

The Roman virtues lift up mortal man.

–Addison, Cato 1.4

In our introduction to *The Lawgivers*, we spoke of the role of "given" law in establishing the identity and forming the character of a people. In his *Lives of Phocion of Athens* and *Cato the Younger of Rome*, Plutarch depicts two men who were viewed by their fellow citizens as the fully formed models of their societies. The ideals they embraced, the virtues they embodied, the codes they lived by— no one could find fault with any of these, but because of the times in which they lived, they were regarded as old-fashioned and out of date. The traditional Greek and Roman norms were no longer the norm. Nonetheless, by virtue of their unbending integrity and strength of character, both men played key roles in the events of their day and remained for future generations heroic figures for endeavoring to preserve their country and its ideals when these were threatened with extinction.

1

We might describe the Lives of Phocion and Cato the Younger as noble tragedies, the stories of men who were overwhelmed by fortune, as Plutarch might have said, or by history, as we tend to say today. Both stories rise to a climax and exhibit their finest literary qualities in their death scenes, and both death scenes explicitly echo the death of Socrates, the "cult hero" of Plutarch's beloved Academy. And "cult hero" is not an inappropriate term to describe Cato, either. Cato had already been treated as such immediately after his death by the remaining Republicans and would continue to be revered as such under the Empire. (See for example our note on Thrasea Paetus in section [25]).

The case of Phocion is less obvious. That he was rehabilitated shortly after his death is certain, but Plutarch's treatment seems to be fairly unique. In any case, it is largely thanks to Plutarch's Lives that both figures regained a kind of cult status in the seventeenth and eighteenth centuries in Europe and America, Cato for his defense of Liberty and Republicanism, and Phocion for his Stoicism and the Federalist cause in America.

Indeed, it would be hard to over estimate the influence of Plutarch's *Life of Cato* on the generation of America's Founding Fathers. George Washington, it is said, modeled himself after the Roman senator and over the course of his lifetime became intimately familiar with the play *Cato* by Joseph Addison based on Plutarch's biography. This play was first performed in London in 1713 and found enthusiastic audiences throughout the century that followed, especially in the New World. The letters and speeches of the time are peppered with quotations from the play, and it is said that Washington had it performed for his soldiers at Valley Forge in spite of a congressional resolution forbidding the performance of plays as harmful to republican virtue. The American historian David McCullough believes that Patrick Henry drew his inspiration for "Give me Liberty or give me death!" from the words in Act II, Scene 4 of Addison's play, "It is not now time to talk of aught/But chains or conquest, liberty or death." From Act IV, Scene 2, he identifies the words "What a pity it is/That we can die but once to serve our country" with Nathan Hale's valediction, "I only regret that I have but one life to lose for my country." The influence of Cato was everywhere. In his life of Washington, Garry Wills reports that two new plays about Cato were being performed in Paris during the first year of the French Revolution, 1789.

If we compare the *Lives* of Phocion and Cato with the *Lives* of the lawgivers Lycurgus and Numa, we are immediately struck by important differences. In Plutarch's narrative, Lycurgus and Numa are virtually masters of events. They control and shape their societies with regard to the future, and what we learn is in the form of a legacy, what Sparta and Rome owed them. Phocion and Cato, on the other hand, while playing key roles, do so in opposition to more powerful figures that influence events far more profoundly than they. They are the losers in their stories, and loss itself engulfs them—lost opportunities, lost friends and countrymen, lost freedoms, and lost hopes.

Moreover, while the stories of Lycurgus and Numa are largely legendary, the events narrated in the *Lives* of Phocion and Cato are for the most part well documented. We have contemporary firsthand accounts, which in many cases come from a perspective far different from that of Plutarch's protagonists. As a consequence of these differences, we are invited when reading these *Lives* to consider how the other major actors viewed these events as well as to see the events themselves in a wider historical perspective: past, contemporary, and future.

II
True fortitude is seen in great exploits
That justice warrants, and that wisdom guides,
All else is tow'ring frenzy and distraction.
–Addison, Cato 2.1

We are calling this volume of Plutarch's *Parallel Lives The Statesmen*. A statesman is a politician who puts the well-being of his country above personal well-being, who, like Plato's philosopher-king, understands the predicament and potential of his fellow citizens and sees it as his duty to serve them. Again and again in his *Lives* of Phocion and Cato, Plutarch endeavors to demonstrate that his protagonists did just that, at a cost, ultimately, of their lives. This is not to say that they were always right in their perception of what was best for their countries or even that they did not on occasion fail. In fact, the moment that may best capture Plutarch's vision of a statesman is when he criticizes Phocion for such a failing. After quoting Phocion's echo of a moral principle found in Plato's *Gorgias*, "I would prefer to suffer an injustice rather than be a party to committing one," Plutarch writes:

> *Although coming from a private citizen this might sound like a high-minded and noble sentiment, upon reflection, I think it ought to give us pause. Inasmuch as he put his country in danger and uttered it as its leader and general, I wonder if he did not transgress a greater and more sacred form of justice owing his fellow citizens...* (*Phocion* 32).

Are statesmen then doomed to fail as these *Lives* might suggest? Might this be Plutarch's not-so-hidden message? Perhaps. The tone of these tales is certainly fatalistic, and it is true that Plato's philosopher-king is, for Plutarch, probably the closest equivalent to what we think of when we call someone a statesman. In the world as it is depicted in Plato's Allegory of the Cave, such a man's chances of success are slim indeed. As Socrates imagines the philosopher who has climbed from our "real world" of shadows and false appearances inside the cave to the blinding light of truth outside and now contemplates returning to serve his fellow citizens as a "statesman," he asks:

4

Suppose there had been honors and citations those below bestowed upon one another, ... do you think he would covet such awards? ... Further, if anyone tried to release the prisoners [of false appearances in the cave] *and lead them up* [to the light of truth] *and they could get their hands on him and kill him, would they not kill him?* (*Republic* vii.516c–517a, Sterling and Scott, 211)

Reading these Lives encourages us to question and refine our own notion of what distinguishes a statesman from a politician. This distinction plays into a number of other questions important for the citizen to work out. What does it mean to love our country rightly? Where do we draw the line between individual liberty and the powers of government? When is flexibility a virtue, and what are the beliefs we should hold even in the face of death?

In an attempt to broaden our readers' perspectives and shed light on the positions of the other actors in this historical drama, we have included in an Appendix several short selections from their firsthand accounts of the events described by Plutarch. Not only will these accounts place a different interpretation upon these events, they will sometimes challenge or contradict Plutarch's facts. Of course, this happens in modern journalism as well. How might one account for these differences? Are the historical circumstances described in these accounts such that the statesman or the man of principle is bound to fail?

III
"My life is grafted on the fate of Rome."
Addison, Cato 2.2

What then were the historical circumstances that brought Phocion and Cato into the spotlight? In the case of Phocion, it was the rise of Macedon, led by Philip and later Alexander the Great, and the failure of the independent Greek city-states to unite. In the case of Cato, it was the concentration of enormous power in the hands of generals like Pompey and Caesar and the inability of a fossilized republican form of government to unite the state and resist these powerful players. Both sets of circumstances resulted in what are arguably the two most significant developments in the history of the ancient Western world.

The Hellenistic kingdoms Alexander established in the former Persian Empire, extending from Egypt and Greece in the west to Bactria (modern Afghanistan, Tajikistan, and Uzbekistan) in the east, would establish a common ruling culture and language, Koine Greek, that would continue to dominate in the Byzantine Empire and only disappear from places like Alexandria and Asia Minor in the twentieth century. In terms of its culture, Greece might even be said to have conquered its savage conqueror Rome, as the Roman poet Horace so memorably put it, and that victory may be said to endure in our schools and institutions today. That spread in turn was the legacy of the Roman Empire, an empire that looked back to Caesar as its founder, giving his name to its rulers and ultimately bestowing that legacy to Russian Czars and German Kaisers.

It is often said that history is told by the victors. But as told by ancient historians, the contrary was more often the case for these two developments, and Plutarch's account is no exception. Possibly because of this, one of the remarkable things about the Roman Empire was the way in which it tolerated, even nurtured, republican sentiment, preserved vestiges of republican institutions, continued to celebrate republican "heroes," and subscribed to republican "virtues" in its Stoic precepts. Accordingly, these *Lives* give us an invaluable and passionate glimpse into a side of the story we can lose sight of if we only follow the trail of the political winners, namely, what was lost.

Both *Lives* involved a new and profound loss of independence and freedom for the men, like Phocion and Cato, who were full citizens of the city-states of Athens and Rome. In the *Life of Phocion* the loss of Athenian freedom is grisly and explicit as the successors of Alexander take charge. The city-state as it had been conceived by Plato and Aristotle and "the freedom which the Greeks as a race had enjoyed for more than a thousand years" [Hammond 651] were suddenly things of the past.

The case of Rome is more complicated. What was Rome? A city, a state, a country, an empire? The words used by Plutarch, *polis* or *pragmata,* can mean any one of these depending on the context. The story told by Plutarch of Cato as a little boy being dangled from the window by the Italian friend of his stepfather is instructive in this regard. The little boy's stubborn reaction to the Italian's demand for the Roman franchise is in fact of a piece with his entire life. For the likes of Cato, Rome was governed in the Forum. It was the affair of men like himself, almost exclusively of Patrician or Plebeian families, climbing the political ladder (their *cursus honorum*), who, when they were not serving as officers in the army or in a provincial administration abroad, would walk to the Forum on a daily basis to conduct Rome's business. The fate of Rome was not yet decided on the Rhine, the Danube, the Bosporus, or some other frontier, although the Civil Wars were beginning to change that, too. Of course, we can be critical of the severe limitation of the franchise in city-states like Athens and Rome, but it is less comforting to remind ourselves of how easily we distance ourselves from our own government and decline responsibility for its actions.

Phocion and Cato *were* Athens and Rome. In them, we see the ripe fruits of two marvelous and complex civilizations fall to the ground as their trees are shaken by the winds of change.

CSH/DVH

TURNING ANCIENT GREEK INTO MODERN ENGLISH

We have undertaken this translation of biographies selected from Plutarch's *Parallel Lives* at the request of CiRCE, the publisher. As with our earlier translations of Marcus Aurelius' so-called Meditations, *The Emperor's Handbook* (Scribner 2002), and the first volume in this series, *The Lawgivers* (CiRCE 2019), Scot starts by making a "raw" translation as close as possible to the original Greek text. Working from Scot's translation and sometimes after consulting other translations, David seeks to produce a translation that reads smoothly in English and conveys the meaning (and as much of the nuance as possible) of Plutarch's prose. In this way, we hope we have made a translation friendly to students of all ages.

Plutarch's vocabulary is probably the richest of any of the ancient prose writers. Typically, the vocabulary judged suitable for Greek prose was much more restrictive than that for the poets, but Plutarch wrote prose with the flair and freedom of a poet. This makes him difficult to translate but fun to read. Many of our words in English have their roots in ancient Greek. We have tried to respect this fact and retain some of the Greek words in the text when we could not find a good English equivalent or when we think it's a term our cosmopolitan readers will want to add to their own vocabularies.

Part of making our translation "student-friendly" was adding words and phrases to passages that allude to persons and events with which Plutarch's readers would have been familiar but would be unfamiliar to most readers today. In these cases, we have either offered an explanation in our notes or incorporated this information into the text itself.

Ancient Greek may be the richest and most expressive language in the world. Such a supple, flexible, nuanced language is hard to capture in what Churchill liked to call our simple, noble English tongue. Greek sentences are composed of phrases and clauses linked by particles and layered on one another in a way that continually speaks and adds to the main idea while creating a unified whole. There is in this something beautifully reflective of nature as captured by the naturalist John Muir who famously said, "When we try to pick out anything by itself, we find it hitched to everything else in the universe." It was easier for earlier English translators of ancient Greek to replicate this type of complex, cumulative sentence structure. For example, a translation containing the long periodic sentences constructed of dependent clauses typical of English prose during the reign of Queen Victoria may come closer to the style of Plutarch, but this style is difficult and no longer pleasant for most modern readers. A modern translation, we therefore believe, will contain shorter sentences, rendering dependent clauses as independent clauses while using transitions familiar to English speakers to link these shorter sentences and produce the cumulative effect.

This is probably more than you wanted to know, but it will give you some appreciation for what's going on backstage as you enjoy the play. And enjoy the play, we hope you will.

CSH/DVH

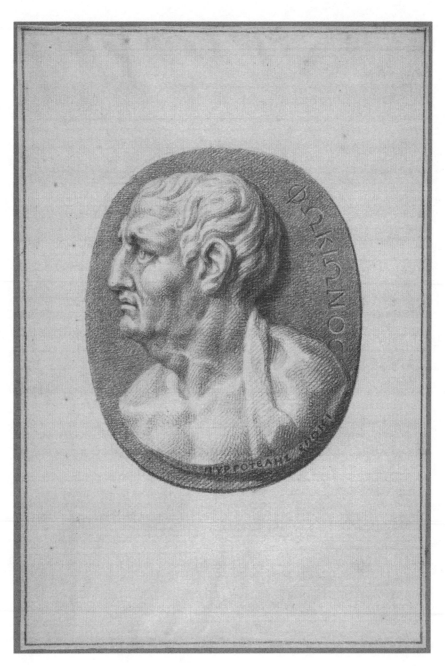

Presumed portrait of Phocion
Bernard Picart, *Paris, 1673–1733*. *The Met Collection*.

The Life of
Phocion of Athens

[1] When the orator Demades became powerful in Athens by ingratiating himself to **Antipater** and the Macedonians and saying and writing many things contrary to the proud character of the city, he excused himself by claiming that he was piloting a shipwrecked state. There would be more truth to this insolent claim if it were applied to the leadership of Phocion. For Demades was himself the shipwreck of Athens, having lived and governed so dissolutely that Antipater said of him in his old age that he was **like an animal sacrifice picked to bits with nothing left but tongue and guts**. The **virtue** and brilliance of Phocion, on the other hand, overmatched by the violent times in which he lived and overshadowed by the misfortunes of Greece, are largely obscured and forgotten. Sophocles goes too far when he underestimates the strength of virtue by saying in the ***Antigone***,

> *When trapped by evil circumstances, O King,*
> *Even the wise lose common sense and act like fools.*

This much, however, we can allow: that when **Fortune** is aligned against good men, it has the power to weaken their *reputation* for virtue and reward them with public disgrace and slanderous abuse rather than the honors and gratitude they deserve.

[2] Although it is commonly assumed that when people are puffed up with power and prosperity, they are more prone to abuse good men, the opposite is in fact the case. Hard times embitter the characters and sour the minds of men, rendering them quick-tempered and easily offended. They are apt to take offense at any expression of honest opinion. And any criticism, however well-intentioned, is received as an insult, and speaking frankly is taken for ridicule. Just as **honey** causes bodily pain when applied to wounds and ulcers, so words that are truthful and sensible, if not offered in a gentle and conciliatory manner, often sting those who are going through hard times. Surely this is why **the poet** calls sweetness "spirit-soothing," because it yields to what pleases the soul and does not fight or resist it. A swollen eye prefers dark colors and lingering in the shade while shunning bright colors and sunlight. Just so the State experiencing misfortunes is in its

[1] Antipater: See Introduction for the historical setting to Phocion's career. Antipater was a Macedonian general under Philip II and acted as a regent of the empire after the death of Alexander the Great.

Like an animal sacrifice picked to bits with nothing left but tongue and guts: In ancient practice, the meat of sacrificial victims was eaten in a sacrificial feast. Antipater's jibe aimed at the orator's reputation for intemperance and fine dining.

Virtue or exellence: Both words translate the Greek *aretē*, a word at the heart of Plutarch's project in his *Parallel Lives,* but often difficult to translate into a single word in English. Like *virtus,* its Latin equivalent, its original association is to manly qualities in a society of warriors. The Italian use of *virtù* in the Renaissance is perhaps the closest modern equivalent. In ancient Greek *aretē* gradually comes to include what we would call the civic and moral virtues. Indeed, Phocion (nicknamed "the Good") and Cato the Younger are chosen precisely for these virtues. But in terms of this same *aretē* Plutarch will choose—and would have considered it absurd not to choose—to write the parallel lives of their counterparts, Alexander the Great and Julius Caesar, warriors *sine qua non,* whose moral and civic virtues, inasmuch as they demonstrated them, are far overshadowed by their sheer ambition (to be number one) and achievement (of world dominion).

Antigone: These lines are spoken by Antigone's sister Ismene to King Creon. It might strike us as odd that Plutarch would assign this thought to Sophocles, when it is clearly put into the mouth of a character that, in context, unlike her sister, is cowering before authority.

Fortune: The cult of Latin *Fortuna,* Greek *Tyche,* was popular in Hellenistic Greece and in Rome. Her role in history as the cause of natural phenomena is common in the historian Polybius.

[2] Honey: well known by the ancient Greeks as a source of healing. Plutarch's metaphor compares it to the "truthful and sensible" words, not the "gentle and conciliatory" words as our association with its sweetness might lead us to believe.

The poet: i.e., Homer.

PD-US ⓒⓒ

The Tyche of Antioch, *a marble copy of a bronze by Eutychides (a name meaning "child of Good Fortune") in the Vatican Museum.*

13

weakness too sensitive to accept frank and honest counsel when it is most needed and when the consequence of ignoring it most disastrous. These are dangerous times for the State as well as for those who attempt to lead it. They destroy both **the one who flatters it after first destroying the one who refused to flatter it**.

Mathematicians tell us that the sun's movement in the heavens is neither predictable nor fixed. Nor is it entirely unpredictable and arbitrary. Rather, it descends on an elliptical path, winding round and round in a pliant and flexible spiral, dispersing its light in a manner that preserves nature and promotes growth. Likewise, in politics, a path that is too fixed and inflexible and opposed to popular opinion is bound to be resented by the people whereas the path of popular opinion that the majority **fall prey to** is a slippery slope dragging both leaders and followers downhill to danger and disaster. Making concessions in response to those whom the leader wishes to persuade based upon what is in the public interest and for the common good—this is the safe path of a true statesman. (Humans will serve willingly and put up with much if they are not ordered around and treated like slaves.) This takes great effort and patience. Admittedly, it isn't easy to mix what is right with what is conciliatory; however, the right mixture, when achieved, makes **beautiful music**. Indeed, these are the same melodious rhythms and harmonies by which God is said to govern the world, not through the use of force but achieving his purposes by means of persuasion and reason.

[3] This description fits Cato the Younger as well. He, too, was no crowd pleaser and possessed manners unlikely to win him any popularity contests. Nor was his public life built by handing out favors. Cicero once said of him that he failed to obtain the consulship by campaigning as though he were in Plato's Republic rather than in **Romulus' sewer**. I would say that he suffered the same fate as fruit that ripens out of season: remarkable and pleasing to the eye but inedible. In like manner, Cato's old-fashioned virtues, appearing as they did many years later in a decadent and depraved society, may have brought him fame and glory, but the gravity and greatness of his virtue were utterly unsuited to the demands of his times. His country was not like Phocion's, already capsizing, but the ship-of-state was tempest-tossed. He managed to lay ahold of the sheets and stays, but in competition with **much more powerful men,** he was thrust from the helm. All

The one who flatters it after first destroying the one who refused to flatter it: i.e., Demades and Phocion in the case of Athens.

Mathematicians: For the ancient Greeks, the designation covered a wide range as the term scientists does for us today.

Fall prey to: Plutarch's point is fine and easy to miss in translation. His verb here, *synepirrepo*, would translate literally as "incline downwards together" and nicely captures those policies around which majorities form in haste only later to regret.

Beautiful music: Plato refers to the governance of the cosmos as a harmony in the *Timaeus*, a notion that is thought to have derived from Pythagoras and comes to be known as *Musica Universalis* or Music of the Spheres in the Renaissance.

[3] Romulus' sewer: Cicero's point is nice when we remember that Rome's main sewer line, the *cloaca maxima*, ran from the Roman Forum to the Tiber River.

Much more powerful men: notably Pompey and Caesar.

the same, he put up a courageous fight against Fortune. She used others to bring down the Republic, but only after a long, slow, arduous struggle in which it very nearly survived owing to Cato and Cato's virtue.

It is the peculiar quality of Cato's virtue, not the general similarities between good men and public figures, that makes Cato and Phocion a fit comparison. There is undoubtedly a difference between one courage and another, between that of Alcibiades and that of Epaminondas, between one intelligence and another, between that of Themistocles and that of Aristides, between the justice of Numa and the justice of Agesilaos. But in the case of Phocion and Cato, up to the minutest detail their virtues display one character, one shape, one tone, one common and indistinguishable combination of traits, as if an equal measure of gentleness had been mixed to match their severity, of courage to match their caution, of extreme concern for the safety of others to match their utter disregard for the safety of themselves, of hatred of evil harmoniously matched with zeal for justice. In short, it would take the subtlest of reasoning to discern a particle of difference between their virtues.

[4] **Cato is known to have belonged to an illustrious family**, of which we shall speak in due course, and I'm confident that Phocion's family was not at all ignoble or obscure, either. If indeed he was the son of a **pestle-maker**, as **Idomeneus** reports, this disparaging fact would not have been omitted from the speech in which Glaucippus, son of Hyperides, uttered thousands of insults against him. Nor indeed would Phocion, while just a lad, have enjoyed the **freedom** to pursue a liberal education under Plato and later Xenocrates at the Academy where he devoted himself from the beginning to the noblest pursuits. He demonstrated such **composure** that rarely did any Athenian ever see him laughing or crying. He seldom used the public baths, according to Douris of Samos, and he always carried **his hand inside his cloak** when he wore one. Whether walking through the countryside or on a military campaign, he went barefoot and lightly clad unless it was unusually and unbearably cold. His fellow soldiers used to joke that it was a sign of a hard winter when Phocion wore a cloak.

[4] Cato is known to have belonged to an illustrious family: an allusion to his famous great grandfather, Marcus Porcius Cato, whom we refer to as Cato the Elder. Cato the Elder is especially famous for ending his speeches in the Senate, regardless of the topic, with the words, *Karthago delenda est!*—Carthage must be destroyed!

Pestle-maker: It was a common practice to denigrate a political rival by calling him the son of an artisan or merchant. The fifth century Athenian demagogue Cleon was called a tanner and was parodied in Aristophanes' *Knights* as a sausage-vendor. Octavian (the future Augustus) was supposed to be the grandson of an African baker and perfume-maker. And the Emperor Vespasian was called the son of a bricklayer. Now the fact that his family, the Flavians, had made their fortune in bricks, of which Rome was in fact built, puts things in perspective.

Idomeneus: Idomeneus of Lampsacus was an early disciple of Epicurus. Along with Douris of Samos below and Chares of Mytilene, a courtier of Alexander the Great, in section seventeen, he is one of the three sources cited by Plutarch in his life of Phocion. For the main lines of Phocion's story, however, Plutarch's sources evidently go unnamed.

Freedom: Our translation of the Greek phrase could be more literally translated `liberal lifestyle`: liberal as in liberal education, an education befitting a free person, i.e., free from having to earn one's living. On this notion common to the Greek and Roman elite, see for example Plutarch's life of Lycurgus [24] (Hicks and Hicks 86–87).

Composure: The description that follows is one that would conjure up for Plutarch's readership the old-fashioned manners reminiscent of descriptions of Solon of Athens, for example, much in the same way that he described Cato's `old-fashioned virtues` in the previous section, and used the Greek term *baros*, the equivalent of the Latin *gravitas*, a term that we still use today to speak of a leader's serious and dignified composure.

His hand inside his cloak: in other words, affecting the style of ancient orators, who refrained from gesturing when they spoke.

[5] Although he was exceedingly kind and gentle, he wore such a dour and stern expression that those unfamiliar with him rarely approached him alone. When once **Chares** provoked Athenian laughter by poking fun at Phocion's frowning looks, Phocion responded by saying, "My frowns have never harmed anyone, whereas the laughter of these men has often made you weep." In similar fashion, Phocian's speech, pithy and authoritative, trenchant and without embellishment, always contained some wise observation or instruction. As **Zeno** said, a philosopher's words ought to be bathed in thought before they are uttered. Just so, Phocion's speech packed a maximum of thought in a minimum of words. This is probably what **Polyeuctus of Sphettus** meant when he said that Demosthenes was the best orator but Phocion the most formidable. For Phocion, it wasn't the length of the speech or the size of the coin that mattered, but its intrinsic worth. He was once observed, they say, pacing backstage deep in thought while **the theatre** was filling up when a friend remarked, "Phocion, you look like you're pondering something." "By Zeus I am," he said. "I'm wondering what I can cut from the speech I'm about to deliver to the Athenians." When Phocion rose to speak, Demosthenes, who famously looked upon all other speakers with contempt, would say quietly to his friends, "Here comes my speech's pruning knife." This comment, however, may be a reference to Phocion's character rather than his oratory, since a single word, even a gesture, from a highly esteemed person is more potent than a thousand clever arguments and a polished delivery.

[6] As a young man, Phocion attached himself to the general Chabrias, from whom he learned a lot about waging war while, in return, acting as a bridle on the general's sometimes impulsive and mercurial behavior. Usually phlegmatic and not easily aroused, once in battle, Chabrias would spring to action, his courage ablaze, and rush headlong into danger with the boldest. This is exactly what eventually cost him his life in Chios, advancing with his **trireme** ahead of the fleet to force a landing. But Phocion, being both calm and resolute, knew when and how to rouse the general when he was being lackadaisical and how to rein him in when being impulsive. For this reason, the kind-hearted and noble Chabrias loved him much and made sure that Phocion was given many opportunities to lead and see action and assume important roles and become known

[5] Chares: one of the Athenian generals, or *strategoi*, who led the Athenians on several campaigns until their final defeat by the Macedonians at Chaeronea in 338 BC, after which he served for the Persian king in Asia Minor. In the Classical period, the Athenian assembly elected ten *strategoi* every year.

Zeno: the founder of Stoicism.

Polyeuctus of Sphettus: a contemporary and supporter of Demosthenes.

The theatre: the Athenian assembly was often held in the Theater of Dionysus as an alternative to the Pnyx. Named after the city's Dionysian festival that it was built to house, it was cut into the southern face of the Acropolis and could accommodate as many as seventeen thousand spectators.

The Theater of Dionysus as it appears today, a partial restoration of the Roman reconstruction. PD-US ©

[6] Trireme: The Greek trireme was the aircraft carrier or nuclear submarine of its time, the piece of military hardware that generally proved decisive in battle, enabling, for example, Themistocles' relatively small Greek fleet of triremes to defeat the Persian Armada at Salamis. It was roughly 120 feet in length and contained 170 rowers on three levels, thranite, zygian, and thalamian. Although its upper deck could accommodate hoplites (soldiers like Marines for boarding other ships or going ashore), its principal means of doing battle was the barely submerged battering ram at its bow. The trireme's captain would maneuver his fast-moving ship to strike an enemy ship in its flank and immediately withdraw, sinking the enemy vessel and drowning all those aboard who could not swim.

The Olympias, *a trireme reconstruction executed by the Royal and Hellenic navies and now a ship of the Hellenic Navy at dry dock in Piraeus. One of the translators served as a thranite (outrigger oarsman) during the 1990 Sea Trials test of this trireme in the Saronic Gulf. (Photo taken by Christos Templar52)* PD-US ©

The Lenormant Relief, from the Athenian Acropolis, depicting the rowers of an Athenian trireme, ca. 410 BC. Found in 1852, it is one of the main pictorial testaments to the layout of the trireme. By Marsyas (2006), CC BY-SA 2.5, https://commons.wikimedia. org/w/index.php?curid=479132

among the Greeks. In **the naval battle off Naxos**, for example, he made it possible for Phocion to win not a little fame and glory by giving him command of the left wing where the fighting was fierce and the victory quick and decisive. Since this was the first naval battle the Athenians won over the Spartans on their own after the surrender of their city, the victory reinforced the reputation of Chabrias and secured Phocion's reputation as an able commander. Because this victory took place at the time of the **Great Mysteries,** Chabrias celebrated it every year by distributing wine to the Athenians on the sixteenth day of Boedromion.

[7] After this, Chabrias sent Phocion with an escort of twenty ships to collect the **island levies** needed to underwrite the cost of the war. Phocion declined the escort, however, saying that if he were being sent to fight, he would need a larger force, but if to allies, a single ship would suffice. So he sailed off in his lone trireme to visit the islands and parley with their leaders in a calm and friendly manner. Later, he returned with numerous ships sent by the allies to transport their tithes to Athens.

Not only did he serve and honor Chabrias while he was still alive, but even after his death, Phocion remained close to his family and tried to do right especially by his son Ctesippus, a stupid and headstrong fellow whom Phocion hoped would turn out to be a good man. To this end, he corrected him when he needed it and otherwise tried to make allowance for **his faults**. Nevertheless, once while on a military campaign, the troublesome young man would not stop badgering him, peppering him with idle questions and inane opinions concerning how the war should be fought. Phocion was finally heard to exclaim, "O Chabrias, Chabrias! What a costly favor of friendship it is to put up with your son!"

Phocion observed that the men who administered public affairs were divided into two camps as if by lots: the army and the assembly. As if by mutual agreement, neither camp interfered with the claims of the other. There were those who spoke in public and proposed decrees, like Eubulus, Aristophon, Demosthenes, Lycurgus, and Hyperides; while others like Diopeithes, Menesthes, Leosthenes, and Chares gained power with generalships and by waging war. Phocion, on the other hand, wished to restore the system of government as it had existed during the times of Pericles, Aristides, and Solon when both functions were

The naval battle off Naxos: This battle took place in 376 BC when Phocion was twenty-six years old. Chabrias commanded the Athenian right and Cedon the Athenian left wing. When Cedon was killed and the left began to crumble, Chabrias sent a reinforcement of twenty ships under Phocion, who procured the Athenian victory. Athens had defeated the Spartan fleet using Persian ships at Cnidos in 394 BC, but, as Plutarch says, this was the first naval battle the Athenians won with their own fleet since Lysander's capture of the town in 403 BC to conclude the Second Peloponnesian War.

Great Mysteries: the Great Mysteries was the major celebration of the Eleusinian Mysteries, which took place from the 14th to the twenty-third of Boedromion, a lunar month falling at the end of summer. It was the most important religious event in ancient Greece, involving the cult of Demeter and Persephone, and so with the mysteries of life, death, and rebirth.

[7] Island levies: The historical context here is known as the Second Athenian League or Second Athenian Confederacy (378–355 BC), a revival of the Delian League of the century before. The earlier league began as a defensive alliance against Persia whereas the later league was started as a defensive alliance against Sparta. In both cases Athens demanded contributions or collected levies from island states to defray naval expenses, and in both instances the levies became increasingly unpopular with Athenian allies. Plutarch's account of Phocion's success at collecting the levies is plausible given the early date, but it is no doubt embellished. [See especially section 11 below.]

His faults: Other sources confirm that Ctesippus' faults were the subject of public ridicule.

harmoniously united. These men showed themselves to be, in the words of the poet Archilochus,

> *Gifted in both arms and arts*
> *And friends alike of **Enyalios** and the Muses.*

Nor did Phocion fail to recognize in Athena, whose name their city bore, **both a goddess of wisdom and of war**.

[8] Positioned thus, Phocion always pursued a policy of peace and calm while at the same time serving as general not only more often than any man in his own day but also more than any general in former times. Although he never sought or campaigned for the post, he never refused or avoided it either, serving whenever the city asked. Our sources all agree that he served as general forty-five times without ever being present at his election but voted for and summoned in his absence. This, frankly, amazes many people. Why would people choose someone like Phocion who almost always opposed them and never said or did anything simply out of a desire to please them? In truth, just as kings are entertained by jesters and flatterers while **dining**, in like manner, the Athenians enjoyed being entertained by boasting and flattering demagogues. But when it came time to appoint men for serious and important work on behalf of the city, they chose the most austere and thoughtful citizen, regardless of how much he opposed their whims and mood swings.

Phocion freely accepted his contrarian status in Athens. When a Delphic oracle stating that all Athenians, save one, were of the same mind, Phocion promptly stepped forward and told them that they need look no further. He was the man—the only man displeased with everything they were doing. Once when his speech was greeted with cheers and applause in the Assembly, Phocion, turning to some friends standing nearby, said, "What's wrong? Did I say something stupid?"

[9] Another time when the Athenians were soliciting contributions to a public sacrifice and began putting pressure on Phocion to follow the example of others and make a donation, he pointed to the banker Callicles and said, "Why not ask this wealthy

"Enyalios:" son of Ares, or another name for Ares, god of war.

Both a goddess of wisdom and of war: As goddess of wisdom Athena is represented by the Attic owl on her coinage. Athena Promachos ("Athena who fights in front" or "Athena the champion"), is the name of her statue by Phidias on the Acropolis and Athena Polias ("Athena guardian of the city"), the name of her archaic temple on the Acropolis that was destroyed by the Persians in 480 BC.

[8] Dining: The Greek reads literally "after washing their hands," a reference to dining.

The Acroplis at Athens. Leo von Klenze, 1846 PD-US ©

*An idealized view of **Phidias' statue on the Acropolis** by the 19th century German painter Leo von Klenze.*

An Attic tetradrachma *with Athena on the obverse and her owl on the reverse.* PD-US ©

A small bronze replica of Phidias's statue of Athena Promachos as it appears on ancient coins. (The Met) PD-US ©

23

money-lender? **How can I give you money when I haven't paid him back his loan?"** When the crowd kept shouting and heckling him, he answered them with the following **story**: "A certain coward set out for the war, and on the way he heard a pack of crows cawing, so he laid his weapons aside and sat down. Silence. So he picked up his weapons and resumed his journey, but the cawing started up again. This time he stopped for good, saying to the crows, 'Caw as long and as loud as you like, but this day you won't be picking my bones!'"

Another time the Athenians urged him to lead them out to war. When he flatly refused, they began calling him an unmanly coward, and he responded by saying, "Your urging will not make me brave, and my refusal will not make you cowards. None of this changes what we already know about each other."

Once when the city was imperiled, the assembly became exasperated with him and demanded an exhaustive annual review. "My dear friends," he said, "let us first see to the safety of our city."

Another time, after a war during which the Athenians had fought timidly and cravenly—and now that peace had been restored, began to act with overbearing self-assurance and to blame Phocion for having deprived them of victory—he made this reply, "My friends, you are lucky to have a commander who knows you so well. Otherwise, you would have been destroyed long ago."

When the Athenians refused to negotiate **a territorial dispute with the Boeotians** and clamored for war, he advised them as follows: "You would do better to fight with words where you have the edge, rather than with arms where you are the weaker party."

One day when the assembly refused to listen to him and tried to shout him down, Phocion said, "You may force me to act against my better judgment, but you can't stop me from speaking my mind."

On another day, his political opponent Demosthenes warned him, **"One of these days**, Phocion, the Athenians will get angry with you and kill you." "And when they calm down and come to their senses," Phocion replied, "they will kill you."

On a hot, hot day, seeing the very fat Polyeuctus of Sphittus wheezing and perspiring and drinking lots of water while advising the Athenians in assembly to go to war against Philip, Phocion said, "Are you really prepared to go to war with

24

[9] "How can I give you money when I haven't paid him back his loan?": Some scholars interpret this to mean, "I cannot make this gift without borrowing money, or I refuse to borrow money to make this gift." Apparently, at the time of Phocion, as well as later in Plutarch's day, there was much corruption around these solicitations for public sacrifices.

Story: contributed to Aesop.

A territorial dispute with the Boeotians: We have an interesting parallel remark from Phocion's frequent opponent Demosthenes in section twenty-four of his speech *On the Peace*: "We are leaving Thebes in possession of Oropus. And if someone were to ask us why and bid us tell the truth, we would respond: 'So as not to go to war.'"

"One of these days": an anecdote that gains in meaning once we learn their respective fates.

Athena fights the giants from the pediment of the original temple, now in the Akropolis Museum (Athens).

this fellow? How do you reckon, all suited out in armor and carrying a shield, he'll fare against the enemy when he can barely deliver a prepared speech without dying from exhaustion?"

When Lycurgus repeatedly attacked him in assembly for advising the city to hand over to Alexander **the ten citizens** he demanded, Phocion responded, "I have often offered good and helpful counsel to these citizens, but they never took it."

[10] There was a fellow named Archibiades they called "Mr. Sparta." He had a big, bushy beard, always wore a threadbare cloak, and never stopped scowling. One day when Phocion was being attacked in council, he called upon Archibiades to bear witness and come to his aid. So "Mr. Sparta" got to his feet and, while stroking his beard, began telling the Athenians at length just what they wanted to hear. At this, Phocion grabbed him by the beard and said, "O Archibiades, I think you need a shave!"

Aristogeiton, a frequent **accuser**, posed as a mighty soldier in assembly where he was always talking up war, but when the day came to muster the citizens for battle, he showed up with his legs bandaged and leaning on a cane. Phocion, espying him from afar, called out to the recording officer, "Write down, 'Aristogeiton, lame and good for nothing.'"

We may wonder how it is possible for someone with such a gruff and dour personality to acquire an epithet like **"the Good**." Yet though difficult, it is not, I suppose, impossible for a man, like a fine wine, to be both sweet and acidic at the same time, or conversely, to be sweet on the tongue but upsetting to the stomach. Hyperides, it is reported, once said in assembly, "Men of Athens, don't simply accuse me of being harsh, but look into whether I am being paid to be so." His point being that there is nothing wrong with being severe so long as one comes by his severity naturally, and it is not a paid act. By this strange logic, we are asked to excuse those who render themselves odious and obnoxious by giving free rein to their anger and jealousy and other passions so long as they are not being paid for doing so.

Now, Phocion never abused a fellow citizen out of spite or considered him an enemy. It was only when he had to stand up to those who opposed what he proposed for the public good that he became a harsh, unyielding, and determined adversary. Otherwise and at all times, he was **kind to all, impartial, and humane**, even to

The ten citizens: The anecdote refers to the decision that would eventually cost Phocion his life. Lycurgus was among the ten as was Demosthenes. It is not difficult to understand how Phocion's response would strike an Athenian assembly as inadequate. It nonetheless was backed up by the successful embassy he had headed in 335 BC, when Alexander withdrew his earlier demand to hand over those men, including Demosthenes and Lycurgus, who supported the revolt of Thebes (Hammond 601).

[10] Accuser: "the Sycophant" in Greek. In Athens, there was no public prosecutor, so cases had to be brought to court by private citizens. This practice lent itself to libelous prosecutions, and the person who brought them was treated with the vulgar term *sycophant*. In later forms of society, the word easily comes to mean, as it does exclusively in English, "a person who acts obsequiously towards someone important in order to gain advantage" (OED).

"The Good": Ancient Greek had a number of words that are sometimes rendered "good" in English. This one suggests good in the sense of useful or beneficial, and it was used to describe useful or deserving citizens.

Kind to all, impartial, and humane: Three of the words, along with words usually translated, "gentle," kind, mild, sweet, that Plutarch will use repeatedly to describe behavior he admires. A study of this vocabulary—the way it develops, its importance in Greek thought, and the way it culminates in Plutarch—was made by the French Hellenist Jacqueline de Romilly in a book entitled, *La douceur dans la pensée grecque,* : (Paris: Les Belles Lettres, 1979).

the extent of coming to the assistance of his political adversaries when they were in trouble or needed an advocate in court. When his friends once reproached him for defending a criminal in court, he reminded them that the innocent have no need of an advocate. When Aristogeiton, the accuser mentioned above, was sentenced to prison, he begged Phocion to visit him there. When Phocion agreed to go, his friends tried to prevent him.

"My dear friends," he said, *"please let me go. Consider, where better to meet Aristogeiton?"*

[11] Indeed, the allies and islanders treated as an enemy any general other than Phocion sent out by Athens. They would strengthen their fortifications, blockade their harbors, and bring their herds, slaves, women, and children into the city from the countryside. But **as long as Phocion was in command**, they would go out in their boats to meet him, wearing festive crowns and bringing him rejoicing to their homes.

[12] **When Philip made his move on Euboea**, bringing in an army from Macedonia and allying himself with the island's tyrants, **Plutarch of Eretria petitioned the Athenians** to drive out the Macedonians who had occupied the island. Phocion was sent as general with a small force on the assumption that the men of the island would rally to him and swell his ranks. But instead he found himself in grave danger, the country being full of traitors bought off by Philip's **bribery**. He did what he could to secure his forces by taking control of a hill separated from the plain of **Tamynae** by a deep gorge. He concentrated his best soldiers there and instructed his officers to disregard the rest—the whiners and undisciplined, the deserters and disorderly citizens who ran from the camp. In battle, their lack of discipline would make them useless and probably get in the way of the fighting men. **Later, back in Athens,** they would be unlikely to bring actions against him before the assembly owing to the fact that, in doing so, their own bad conduct would come to light.

[13] As the enemy approached, Phocion ordered his men to take up arms but remain in place while he performed the sacrifice which, either

[11] As long as Phocion was in command: This claim recalls the incident recorded in section seven and see note on "island levies" above, sometime shortly after the Battle of Naxos in 376 BC. Plutarch is evidently referring to the period of the Second Athenian League (378–355 BC), but the attitude of the allies to the other commanders suggests a time closer to the so-called Social War (357–355 BC) that marks the league's collapse. Phocion's role in the Social War, if any, is nowhere recorded, and Plutarch's roughly chronological narrative of Phocion's role in historical events begins only in 349 BC in the next section.

[12] When Philip made his move on Euboea: With these words, Plutarch begins his account of Phocion's career from 349 BC until his death in 318 BC. What role did he play from the date of his brilliant debut in 376 until 349 BC, from the age of twenty-six or so to his mid-fifties? Of this we are told nothing. The years covered are the years when Macedon, under Philip, Alexander, and finally Antipater, take control of Greece and the Greece of competing—and constantly warring—city-states disappears. For the modern historian, that process was cemented at the Battle of Chaeronea in 338 BC, but it was already well advanced by the time Philip assumed leadership of the Amphictyonic Council and defeated Phocis in 352 BC. We know from other sources that Phocion and eight thousand mercenaries were employed by Artaxerxes to reduce Cyprus in 350 BC (Hammond 547), but we can only guess that the lines of Phocion's politics, in particular his opposition to Demosthenes' aggressive anti-Macedonian position, only became clear in the years covered. Once again, we are reminded that Plutarch's attention is directed toward illustrating his protagonist's character rather than giving a complete account of his life or inquiring into historical trends such as, for example, the rise of Macedon or the decline of Athens.

Plutarch of Eretria petitioned the Athenians: This event is dated to 349 BC, three years before the end of the Third Sacred War, which pitched the Amphyctionic Council, an ancient association of Greek tribes (now city-states) meant to manage Delphi, against the Greek city-state of Phocis. The Council accused Phocis of cultivating sacred land and imposed a very large fine, which the Phocians refused to pay. Eventually, they even occupied the sacred shrine at Delphi itself to help pay for the war. This war came on the heels of the Social War (357 to 355 BC), which involved the revolt against Athens of states in the Second Athenian League. During the ten-year Third Sacred War, Philip II of Macedon secured control of Thessaly and the gold mines on Mount Pangaion, and he was eventually able to assert his authority on the Amphictyonic Council itself and take over its leadership. The major engagement of the war, known as the Battle of Crocus Field (352 BC), was one of the bloodiest recorded in ancient Greek history. Six thousand Phocian troops were killed and another three thousand captured by Philip and his Macedonians. Inasmuch as this was a "sacred war" to defend Delphi, the Macedonians were crowned with laurel, and the prisoners were killed by hanging or drowning (Hammond 544).

Bribery: The ability of the Macedonians, now Philip but soon in a much more lavish way, Alexander, to buy political allies and the relative impoverishment of Greek city-states and susceptibility to such "generosity" are constant features in the period. Athens, like other Greek city-states, was always hard pressed for funds to support its military ambitions and was in the habit of hiring itself out as a mercenary force. We noted above that Phocion and a force of eight thousand mercenaries were hired by Persia in the year prior to the one under discussion, and the student of Xenophon's *Anabasis*, or *March of the Ten Thousand*, will note how effective and invaluable a fighting force these mercenaries were.

Tamynae: Tamynae was on the south coast of Euboea to the west of Chalcis and Eretria.

Later, back in Athens: Plutarch alludes to the practice of accusing the general's conduct of a campaign before the assembly, a recurrent feature of political life in Greek city-states.

because the initial omens were not clear or because he wished to draw the enemy closer, took a long time. Plutarch mistakenly interpreted this delay as cowardice and rushed out with his **local troops**. Seeing this, the cavalry also poured out of the camp in disorder and tried to engage the enemy. When the enemy crushed the leading edge of this charge, men and horses scattered, and Plutarch himself fled. Thinking they had won the day, the enemy now stormed the palisade and tried to hack it down and breach the walls. But at this moment, the sacrifice having been successfully concluded, the Athenians counter-attacked, throwing back the enemy and killing most of those who fled and sought refuge behind the breastworks. Phocion now ordered a phalanx of hoplites to remain in position so as to receive those who had scattered in flight earlier, and meanwhile, he pressed the battle with his best soldiers. It was a ferocious and bloody affair in which his men fought gallantly and tirelessly. Thallus, the son of Kineus, and Glaucus, the son of Polymedes, distinguished themselves fighting side by side with Phocion himself, but it turned out to be Cleophanes who proved of greatest worth in this battle. By shouting for the cavalry to return and come to the aid of their endangered general, he secured victory for the hard-pressed hoplites. After this, Phocion expelled Plutarch from Eretria and captured the strategic citadel of Zaretra, located at the island's narrowest point with seas on each side. He then released all the Greek prisoners he had taken, fearing that the Athenians, in a fit of anger and goaded on by the assembly's orators, might be persuaded to **treat them badly**.

[14] Having accomplished all this, Phocion sailed home. But it wasn't long before everyone had good reason to regret his absence, the allies for his goodness and humanity, the Athenians for his experience and courage. The man who took his place, Molossus, conducted the war in such a way as to **fall into the hands of the enemy**.

Entertaining high hopes of great things, **Philip now entered the Hellespont** with his entire army and threatened the Cheronese, Perinthus, and Byzantium. When the Athenians raised a force to aid these cities, the popular orators persuaded them to send Chares as commander. Chares sailed into the Hellespont but accomplished nothing worthy of the force at his command. Mistrustful of his

[13] **Local troops**: translating *xenoi* foreigners: which designates anyone not a citizen of one's own city-state. In this case, Plutarch is likely leading Euboean troops. Later in the section, we find that Plutarch may have changed sides or at least is no longer a trusted or reliable ally to Athens. Our author Plutarch, however, seems to indicate that he does not regard Plutarch's move here as premeditated.

Treat them badly: Plutarch uses what amounts to a euphemism here inasmuch as it was not uncommon at the time for prisoners to be sold as slaves or killed. The question of the fate of "fellow" Greeks defeated in battle sharply divided public opinion in the ancient world.

[14] **Fall into the hands of the enemy**: Plutarch is apparently alluding to the story that Athens had to ransom its prisoners for fifty talents, a hefty sum at a time when the treasury was chronically short of funds. At this point, Athens effectively lost control of Euboea.

Philip now entered the Hellespont: For the historian, the crucial piece of information missing from Plutarch's account of Philip's intervention in the Hellespont here is that it was provoked by Athens' alliance with Persia and Artaxerxes' initiative in seeking to assert Persian control on these Greek cities. In other words, Philip could be seen as acting in his role as leader of the Greeks in their defense against Persia (see Hammond 551, 563).

We are in the spring of 340 BC, eight years after the events narrated above. The intervening years witnessed Philip's settlement of the Sacred War in 346 BC, followed by an intense diplomatic struggle between Macedon and Athens and an intense political struggle in Athens between Demosthenes and Aeschines. In his settlement of the Sacred War, Philip had lived up to the hopes of Isocrates as the guarantor of peace and concord among the Greek states, and Demosthenes had silently acquiesced to Philip's proposal for peace and an alliance. But Demosthenes understood that alliance with Macedon ultimately meant subservience to her. His famous speeches, *On the Peace, On the False Legation*, and the second and third *Philippics*, all date from these years, in which he had a preponderant influence on Athenian policy.

In order to give a firsthand glimpse into this political struggle, we have translated in **Appendices A and B** excerpts from Isocrates' discourse addressed to Philip in 346 BC and from Demosthenes' *Third Philippic* delivered in 341 BC. How might Phocion have reacted to these speeches?

motives, the cities refused to allow Chares' fleet into their harbors, so he just wandered from place to place, extorting money from Athens' allies yet despised by its enemies.

Stirred up by the orators back in Athens, the exasperated assembly regretted having tried to aid Byzantium, but, in the midst of this turmoil, Phocion rose to speak and told them that they should not direct their anger at their allies for their mistrust, but at the generals who inspired it. "To command your army you have chosen men who provoke fear even in those friends who know they cannot be saved without your support." Moved by these words, the assembly promptly changed its mind and ordered Phocion himself to command another fleet to aid the allies in the Hellespont. This, more than anything else, is what saved Byzantium, for Phocion was highly respected throughout the Hellespont.

In addition, an old friend of his named Leon, a classmate from their student days together in the Academy, who was renowned among the Byzantines for his virtue, offered the city guarantees on Phocion's behalf. As a result, the city opened wide its gates and allowed him and his army in, and even though he offered to set up his camp outside the city, the Byzantines would hear none of it and invited his soldiers into their homes. Shown so much trust, the Athenians acquitted themselves soberly and blamelessly and fought with great courage in defense of the city. In this way, was Philip driven out of the Hellespont and made, for a time, an object of scorn having until then never been defeated in battle and regarded as invincible. Phocion captured a number of Philip's ships, relieved the towns he had garrisoned, and striking at several locations, plundered and overran his territory until he was wounded and decided to sail home.

[15] On the occasion **when the Megarians secretly called upon him for support**, Phocion, fearing that the Boeotians might get wind of it and attack before he could come to their aid, called an assembly **at dawn**. He explained the situation to the Athenians who promptly voted to aid the Megarians. Wasting no time, Phocion called for the trumpet to summon the people to arms, and he led them out straight from the assembly. The Megarians received them with great joy, and he helped them build two long walls joining Nisaea, the port, to the city. After this, the Megarians had little to fear from their enemies by land and became dependent on Athens.

[15] When the Megarians secretly called upon him for support: The events recounted in this section occurred in 342 BC (*R.E.* see under Phokion), thus two years before those recounted in the previous section. Megara, a city west of Athens on the Saronic Gulf, was throughout the classical period the victim of a tug-a-war between Boeotia and Attica. Like the Piraeus, Nisaea, Megara's port, had been linked to the town by walls (Plutarch calls "legs") in the fifth century BC until they were torn down in 424 BC.

At dawn: Assemblies, in fact, always began at dawn. Plutarch presumably means to say that Phocion summoned an extraordinary meeting of the assembly.

[16] Already the war against Philip was well under way, and other generals besides Phocion had been chosen in his absence. **Upon his return to Athens from the islands**, Phocion pleaded with the assembly—inasmuch as **Philip much preferred peace** and apprehended the dangers of war—to accept the offer of a treaty. But at this point, a chap who liked to hang about **the Heliaea** and make libelous accusations interrupted him saying, "What! You dare to tell the Athenians to lay down the arms they have already taken up?!" "I do indeed," replied Phocion, "even though I know full well that in war I will hold authority over you while in peace you hold it over me." But Phocion could not dissuade his countrymen from wanting war, and instead, they followed Demosthenes who advised them to fight their battles as far away from Attica as possible. "My good friend," said Phocion, "let's not talk about where to fight but rather how to win. To the victors, the battle will seem far away, but to the defeated, it will be at the door."

After **the defeat** at Chaeronea, the **best citizens** took fright when the rabble-rousers and revolutionary elements in the city dragged **Charidemus** to the speaker's platform and called upon him to direct the war. With tears of supplication and the support of the **Council of the Areopagus**, they very narrowly succeeded in persuading the assembly to put Phocion in charge. Phocion counseled his countryman in every respect except one to accept Philip's fair and benevolent terms: they should reject Demades' motion that the city share the same conditions of peace as **the other states in Greece** since they did not yet know what conditions Philip might impose. In the heat of the moment, the assembly ignored his advice but soon came to regret doing so when they learned that they had hastily agreed to a condition of peace requiring them to furnish Philip with cavalry and triremes. "This is what I feared," said Phocion, "when I opposed Demades' motion, but now that the thing is done, let's make the best of it and not lose hope. Remember that our forefathers sometimes ruled and were at other times ruled over, but they always bore their fate nobly and thereby saved themselves and the rest of Greece."

When the news of **Philip's death** arrived, Phocion opposed any show of jubilation or vote of thanksgiving, saying how ignoble it would be to rejoice on such an occasion and reminding his countrymen that the army that had defeated them at Chaeronea was only reduced by a single man.

[16] Upon his return to Athens from the islands: We learn elsewhere that Phocion commanded a fleet attacking Macedonian shipping in the northern Aegean [Hammond 567, and cf. section 14].

Philip much preferred peace: Although this characterizes Philip's behavior until 340 BC, it is difficult to see how it jives with his actions from 340 BC on. He had renounced peace with Athens in 340 BC, and in late 339 BC had moved his armies south, threatening both Boeotia and Attica. The move precipitated an unlikely Theban-Athenian alliance to which many other city-states joined, setting up the confrontation at Chaeronea. That much said, Philip, like his famous son, Alexander, had enormous respect for Athens and saw himself as a proponent and purveyor of Greek culture, which Athens embodied. It is not impossible that Philip's moves were intended to put pressure on Athens to renew the peace and alliance.

The Heliaea: the highest court in Athens. Six thousand jurymen were selected by lots each year, and for any given trial as few as 201 and as many as 1,501 jurors (or *dikasts*) were selected. Jurors received a per diem, subjecting them to the opprobrium of the leisure classes in much the same way as welfare recipients are sometimes regarded today. Plutarch's verb, which we have translated by "hang about," is a likely reflection of this attitude, to which he adds the accusation of sycophancy (for which see note in section [10] above).

The defeat: The Battle of Chaeronea was fought on September 1, 338 BC. It ended in a resounding victory for the Macedonian army against the combined Greek forces led by Athens and Thebes. In the battle, the young Alexander distinguished himself by leading the Macedonian cavalry against the Theban Sacred Band, the elite fighting unit in Greece at this time, and annihilating it.

Best citizens: Like *hoi kaloi k'agathoi* (the noble and good) as opposed to *hoi polloi* (the many), the term used by Plutarch, *beltistoi*, translates the Latin *optimates* and is the way aristocrats referred to their own.

Charidemus: Charidemus of Oreus in Euboea was a mercenary general who had commanded Athenian troops against Philip in the Chersonese in 351 BC.

Council of the Areopagus: the earliest aristocratic council in Athens. The extent of their jurisdiction was limited over time by democratic reforms, but they retained "guardianship of the laws" much as the Supreme Court does in the United States.

The other states in Greece: or Council of the Greeks, also known as the Greek League or the League of Corinth, led by Philip.

Philip's death: Philip II of Macedon was assassinated in 336 BC and succeeded by his son, Alexander the Great.

[17] **To Demosthenes, who was heaping abuse upon Alexander even as the latter was marching against Thebes**, Phocion responded by **quoting from Homer**:

> *"Hothead, why further provoke this savage creature? Why goad him to further acts of self-aggrandizement? Is it truly your wish to throw our city into the fast-approaching conflagration? Those of us charged with saving the city will not consent to seeing it destroyed, no matter how much some may desire it."*

After the destruction of Thebes, when Alexander demanded that the Athenians hand over Demosthenes, Lycurgus, Hyperides, Charidemus, and others, the assembly turned to Phocion and called upon him several times to speak. Finally, he rose, and calling to his side one of his dearest friends, whom he loved and confided in more than anyone else, he said, "These men have put our city in the gravest danger, but even if Alexander demanded my friend Nicocles, I would not hesitate to give him up. Indeed, I would consider it my own good fortune to die in order to save our city." And then he added, "Truly, my fellow citizens, it breaks my heart to see the Thebans who have fled the destruction of their city and sought refuge in Athens. But haven't the Thebans given the Greeks enough to mourn? Is it not now in the best interest of both Greeks and Thebans to placate the victor's wrath and beseech his mercy rather than to risk everything in another battle?"

It is said that when **the first decree** was handed to Alexander, he threw it down and, turning his back on the frightened ambassadors, walked away. But the second decree presented by Phocion he received, having heard from his elders how much his father, Philip, admired the man. Not only did he hear him and grant his petition, he asked for his advice. To this, Phocion responded by saying, "If it's peace you want, you should stop fighting, but if it's glory you're seeking, you should fight against **foreigners** rather than Greeks." Phocion went on to say many other things well suited to the character and desires of Alexander, and, in this way, he so won him over and softened his temper that, in the end, Alexander urged the Athenians to turn their attention to **domestic affairs** and be

[17] To Demosthenes, who was declaiming invective against Alexander when the latter was already marching against Thebes: We are presumably already in 335 BC, sometime before the sack of Thebes in the fall of that year. Demosthenes' celebrated speech, *On the Crown*, which marked his final triumph over Aeschines, was delivered in the previous year when it was rumored that Alexander had been killed in his campaigns on the Danube and in the Balkans, where he was in fact entirely successful. From what Plutarch says here, it is apparent that the mood had changed and that Phocion and like-minded generals had been elected.

[17] Quoting from Homer: This line is quoted from T. E. Shaw's translation of Homer's *Odyssey* ix.494, when Odysseus' companions are trying to prevent him from riling the Cyclops after their narrow escape from Polyphemus' cave. The "hothead," alas, does not take his companions' advice, and they, even more than he, suffer the dire consequences. (The lively translation of T. E. Shaw—better known as Lawrence of Arabia—is well worth looking into.)

After the destruction of Thebes: Thebes was taken and sacked by Alexander and his allies in the Greek League in the fall of 335 BC. Six thousand Thebans were killed, and thirty thousand were taken prisoner. With the approval of the League, Alexander meted out the maximum penalty of *andropodismos*, selling all men, women, and children into slavery, and razing the city to the ground. In a characteristic bow to Greek culture, Alexander decided to spare the house of the Theban poet Pindar.

The first decree: This embassy was headed by Demades, and the decree is said to have congratulated Alexander on his defeat of Thebes (Hammond 602, and for Demades cf. sections one and two).

Foreigners: "barbarians" in Greek; the term they used for peoples who did not speak Greek.

Domestic affairs: Plutarch uses the fairly wide term *pragmata*, like business, that can be used of personal or state affairs. From the context, it would appear that Alexander's remark was the equivalent of our "put your house in order."

prepared to lead Greece should anything happen to him. And on a personal level, he regarded Phocion as a friend and adopted him as a **xenos,** showing him this measure of respect and showering him with honors he bestowed only on the few who were with him at all times. In fact, **Douris** reports that after **his victory over Darius** and he became Great, Alexander stopped addressing his correspondents as "Dear," save for the letters he wrote to Phocion. Only to Phocion and **Antipater** did he condescend to use this intimate form of address. **Chares** also reports this.

[18] Concerning Alexander's lavish generosity, all agree that he once sent Phocion **a hundred talents**. When this gift arrived, Phocion asked those who brought it why in the world Alexander would make such a large gift to just one man when there were so many Athenians. They responded by saying, "Because he regards you to be the only **noble and good** man in the city."

"Well then," said Phocion, "let me ever seem and be so."

Following him into his house and observing his simple manner of living—his wife kneading bread with her own hands and Phocion himself drawing water from the well to clean his feet—they protested even more and insisted that he accept the gift, saying that it was a terrible thing to see the friend of the king living in such poverty. Seeing at that moment an old man in a dirty, worn-out coat pass by, Phocion asked them, "What, do you think I'm worse off than this fellow?"

When they attempted to laugh off this comparison, Phocion became very serious and said, "Listen! This old fellow is perfectly content to live with what he has. If I don't need this money, what is the point in my having it, and if I end up spending it on things I don't need, I'll disgrace both myself and Alexander in the eyes of the Athenians."

So it came to pass that Alexander's lavish gift was sent back to him, showing the Greeks by this simple gesture that richer than the bestower of riches is the one who does not need them. This didn't make Alexander happy, and he wrote back to Phocion saying that he could not consider someone his friend who needed nothing from him. So Phocion seized this opportunity to ask Alexander to free the sophist Echeceratides, Athenodorus of Imbros, and two Rhodians, Demaratus and Sparton, arrested for some reason and imprisoned in Sardis. Alexander immediately granted his request and freed these prisoners. And later, he sent

Xenos: Plutarch uses this technical term for a guest-friend, which amounts to guarantees of inviolable hospitality protected by Zeus. It was a violation of *xenia* that precipitated and justified the Trojan War.

His victory over Darius: The victory over Darius, the Great King of Persia, at Gaugamela in 331 BC effectively made Alexander the ruler over the world as the Greeks knew it—from the Himalayas to the Danube and the Nile and beyond. Had he lived, there is little doubt that he would have added the western Mediterranean to his empire.

Douris . . . Chares: Both Douris, the tyrant of Samos, and Chares of Mytilene, a camp follower of Alexander, might have consulted the collection of Alexander's letters.

Antipater: For Antipater, the Macedonian general who controlled Greece after Alexander's death in 323 BC and eventually the whole of his empire until his death in 319 BC, see section one and sections twenty-three and following.

[18] A hundred talents: One Attic talent represented approximately ten years' wages for a hoplite or a skilled worker in Athens, and a hundred talents equals twice the ransom money demanded for the return of Molossus and the other Athenian prisoners captured in Euboea (see section [14]). As intimated in the next sentence, weighing well over two tons of pure silver, it would have taken a mule train and several drivers to transport. After the conquest of Persia, Alexander commanded resources that beggared the Greek imagination.

"Noble and good": The *kalon k'agathon* expression is used. See note on "best citizens" in section [16] above.

Illustration of Phocion encourting an envoy from Macedon from F. J. Gould, The Children's Plutarch: Tales of the Greeks, *1910 between pp. 132 and 133.*

PHOCION·&·THE·MACEDONION·ENVOY

Craterus to Macedonia, instructing him to offer Phocion **his choice of four cities** in Asia—Cios, Gergithos, Mylasa, or Elaia—and warning Phocion that he would be even angrier if he turned down this gift. But even so, Phocion refused, and Alexander died shortly thereafter.

To this day, Phocion's house in **Melita** is pointed out. Other than the small bronze medallions that decorate it, it is plain and simple and without ornamentation.

[19] Of the women he married, little is known about the first, except that Cephisodotus the sculptor was her brother. Of the second wife, her reputation amongst the Athenians for moderation and frugality was no less than Phocion's for **goodness**. On one occasion when the Athenians were watching **a new tragedy**, the actor who was playing the part of a queen demanded that **the leader of the chorus** provide him with a number of sumptuously attired attendants. When his demand was not met, the actor became peevish and held up the performance by refusing to go on stage. Finally, the leader, Melanthius, hauled him to the center of the stage shouting, "Have you never seen how Phocion's wife always goes out with only **a single maidservant!?** But you have to strut about like a peacock filling our women's heads with foolish notions!" Hearing this speech, the audience broke into loud cheers and applause. Once, when a houseguest, an Ionian woman, was showing Phocion's wife her expensive jewelry, her gold chains and gem-studded necklaces, his wife said, "My jewel is my husband Phocion, now in his twentieth year as Athenian general."

[20] When his son Phocus asked for permission to compete in the **Panathenaic Games as an apobates**, Phocion allowed it, not so much because he cared whether his son might win a prize, but because he thought the discipline and fitness-training would be good for the lad who was otherwise given to excessive drinking and indulgent living. But once his son won, many of his friends wanted to honor him by hosting victory parties. Phocion declined all of these invitations save one, and when he arrived at this party and saw how lavish it was, with even the basins for washing the guests' feet filled with aromatic wine, he called his son to him and said, "How can you allow your friend to spoil the honor of your victory in this way?"

His choice of four cities: This arrangement, for which we have a parallel in the case of Themistocles, gives us an insight into how towns might be expected to provide a livelihood for a distant "patron".

Melita: The deme of Melita was situated near the Agora in Athens.

[19] Goodness: The word alludes to his eponym, Phocion the Good, for which see the note in section ten above.

A new tragedy: At this period, revivals of tragedies from the "golden age" of the previous century were also common.

The leader of the chorus: or *choregos* in Greek. In addition to leading the chorus, the *choregos* served as both producer and director.

"A *single maidservant*": This woman would of course have been a slave, and the anecdote gives us a good sense of how common and numerous slaves were in the ancient world.

[20] Panathenaic Games as an apobates: This is what the Athenians called the young men who jumped from the chariot at the end of the chariot race and ran the stadium race.

And hoping to change completely the young man's habits, he sent him to Sparta and enrolled him in the ranks of the young men undergoing **training** there. The Athenians took offense at this, thinking Phocion was ignoring and despising their local traditions. Demades chided him for this by saying, "Perhaps you'd like Athens to adopt the Spartan constitution? If so, I'm happy to draft a decree to that effect and propose it to the assembly." To this wry suggestion Phocion replied, "Ah, what an excellent idea, Demades! You smelling of myrrh perfume with a fancy cloak slung about your shoulders are just the man to advise the Athenians to sing the praises of Lycurgus while eating Spartan black broth in mess halls!"

[21] When Alexander wrote to demand that the city send him triremes, the usual speakers rose to oppose his demand. When at last the Council asked Phocion to voice his opinion, he said simply, *"I would advise you either to be victorious in battle or to make friends with the victors."* At about this same time there was a chatty, self-important young fellow named Pytheas who was just starting to address the assembly. To him, Phocion directed these words, "Don't you know any better than to keep quiet on a subject of this gravity? **A young slave whom the Demos has just recently acquired** ought to know when to hold his tongue."

When **Harpalus** escaped from Alexander out of Asia, he took with him a great sum of money and came to Attica where he was surrounded by the usual assembly speakers and corrupt politicians hoping to line their pockets by advocating for him. To them, he threw a few crumbs broken off from his vast hoard, but to Phocion, he offered seven hundred talents and anything else he desired, putting himself and his entire fortune at Phocion's disposal. Phocion's gruff response to all this was simply, "Let the plague take him if he doesn't stop corrupting the city!"

For a while this silenced him and put an end to his bribery. But later when the Athenians took up the question of his influence on their city, he saw that those who had taken his money—in order not to be found out—were the very ones who accused him and urged that actions be taken against him. On the other hand, Phocion, who had not taken a penny from him, argued that Harpalus' personal safety was in the public's interest. Seeing this, Harpalus renewed his efforts to

Training: the famed Spartan *agoge*. The Athenian Xenophon did the same for his sons, a not uncommon practice apparently.

[21] *"A young slave whom the Demos has just recently acquired"*. Plutarch employs a term used when buying a slave or a pet. In his translation, Dr. Fowke suggests that this was an old joke amongst the Athenians: to speak of the orators as domestic servants or slaves who flattered, cheated, and misled the Demos, the citizens, their masters.

Harpalus: Harpalus was the treasurer of Alexander, who abandoned him in 324 BC. He came to Athens with five thoursand talents and a force of six thousand mercenaries.

court Phocion's favor, but found him to be like an impregnable fortress besieged on all sides, utterly impervious to bribery. Phocion's son-in-law, Charicles, however, he pulled into his circle of friends, trusting and confiding in him in all that he did and thereby besmirched the young man's reputation.

[22] After the death of his mistress, Pythonica, whom he greatly loved and by whom he had a daughter, Harpalus desired to build a lavish monument and commissioned Charicles to undertake it. Disreputable as this project was on the face of it, **the completed tomb** made it even more shameful. It still stands in Hermeion, on the road between Athens and Eleusis, and nothing in its appearance reflects the sum of thirty talents that Charicles is said to have charged Harpalus for it. When Harpalus himself died, Phocion and Charicles brought up his daughter with great care. And later when Charicles was charged in **the affair of Harpalus** and asked Phocion to plead his case before the court, his father-in-law refused, saying, "I made you my son-in-law, Charicles, only for what is honorable."

Asclepiades, the son of Hipparchus, was the first to announce to the Athenians the news of Alexander's death. Demades, however, dismissed this report saying, "If this were true, the whole world would smell of his rotting corpse!" Seeing that this news had the people all riled up and clamoring for revolution, Phocion attempted to calm them down, but many continued to jump to their feet, demanding to speak and affirm Asclepiades' report, asserting that Alexander was indeed dead. "Surely," said Phocion, "if Alexander is dead today, he will still be dead tomorrow and the day after. This gives us plenty of time to deliberate on the matter calmly and, what is more, with assurance."

[23] When Leosthenes, against Phocion's wishes, sought to plunge the city into the **Hellenic War**, he tried to raise a laugh by asking him mockingly, "Tell us, Phocion, what you have achieved for the city after so many years as her general?"

"It is no small achievement," responded Phocion, "for our citizens to be buried in their family's tombs."

And when Leosthenes continued in his boastful reproaches, Phocion said, "Your speeches, young man, are like cypress trees, impressive and tall but bearing no fruit,"

[22] **The completed tomb**: According to Athenaeus, the monument included a temple and altar dedicated to Pythonica Aphrodite.

The affair of Harpalus: After Harpalus fled Athens and was assassinated in Crete in 323 BC, those who were suspected of having received monies from him were brought to trial.

[23] **Hellenic War**: This war came to be known as the Lamian War (323–322 BC) after its central event, the siege of Antipater in Lamia.

Hyperides then attacked him, demanding to know when he would advise the Athenians to go to war. Phocion's retort: "When I see our young men eager to follow orders, the rich eager to pay taxes, and politicians able to refrain from robbing the treasury."

Later, when many expressed amazement at the size of the force Leosthenes had managed to raise, Phocion was asked what he thought of such impressive preparations. "Fine for a short race," **he said**, "but what I fear is a long race, and our city has nothing left in reserve—neither money, nor triremes, nor hoplites." Events supported his claim. At first, Leosthenes achieved brilliant success, defeating the **Boeotians** in battle and driving Antipater within the walls of Lamia. This early success so intoxicated the citizens of Athens that they celebrated the good news continuously and offered public sacrifices to the gods. Some, perhaps wishing to elicit from Phocion an admission that he had erred in his earlier judgment, asked him if he would not have wished to achieve all this success himself. "Most assuredly, I have wished for it," he said. And again, when more good news arrived from the front, he said, "Will we ever stop winning?"

[24] Leosthenes was killed soon after this, and those who feared that Phocion might succeed him as general and end the war arranged for a relatively ob-scure and unknown fellow to address the assembly. Claiming to be a friend and old school mate of Phocion's, this fellow begged them to spare his in-valuable friend this one time and keep him in reserve and to give command of the army to Antiphilus instead. This proposal pleased the Athenians, but Phocion came forward to say that not only had he never been this man's school mate, he didn't even know him. "But from now on, *mon brave*," said Phocion, "I will consider you to be one of my dearest and closest friends for having proposed what is in my best interest."

The Athenians were hot to march against the Boeotians, but Phocion at first counseled them against it. When his friends told him that they feared the Athenians would kill him for repeatedly opposing their wishes, Phocion replied by saying, "That would be unjust if I have given them good advice, but if not, they have every right to do so." Then, seeing that he could not dissuade them and that they

He said: This anecdote is also attributed to Demosthenes.

Boeotians: After the sack of Thebes by Alexander, the Boeotians had returned to their alliance with Macedon.

persisted in demanding loudly that he should lead them out, he ordered the herald to call up all Athenians from **ephebate** to age sixty and commanded them to pack five days of provisions and follow him at once into the field. This sparked a huge outcry, especially from the **veterans** who leapt to their feet raising fierce objections. "What's the problem?" Phocion asked. "Your eighty-year-old general will be leading you!" In this way, he calmed them down and at least for the moment made them change their minds.

[25] Phocion led the Athenians against Micion who had landed a large army of Macedonians and mercenaries at Rhamnonte and from there was ravaging the land all along the coast of Attica. Meanwhile, he was plagued on all sides by those self-important persons advising him to take a certain hill or to make a cavalry charge or to form a battle line until finally he cried out, "By Herakles! I see plenty of generals, but where are my soldiers?" When at last he formed a battle line, one of his hoplites, wishing to show his courage, ran ahead of the rest, but upon seeing the enemy, he returned quickly to the line. "Young man," said Phocion, "are you not ashamed to have disobeyed two orders in a single day—first by deserting the line where your general placed you, and second by retreating from where you placed yourself?" Nevertheless, Phocion routed the enemy, putting it to flight and killing Micion and many of his soldiers.

At this time, the Greek army in Thessaly—the phalanx commanded by Antiphilus, the cavalry by the Thessalian Menon—also defeated Antipater, who had been joined by Leonnatus and the Macedonians from Asia. Leonnatus was slain.

[26] Shortly after this, Craterus crossed from Asia with a huge force and this time defeated the Greeks in Thessaly at Krannonas. This battle, however, was neither decisive nor one in which the Greeks suffered heavy losses. Nevertheless, owing either to their mistrust of their young and overly indulgent commanders or to the machinations of Antipater who was plotting to undermine their political support from the cities, the Greek army dispersed and shamefully surrendered the **liberty** of the Greek states. Antipater now turned his attentions on Athens. Upon hearing the news of his approaching army, Demosthenes and Hyperides

[24] *Ephebate*: The *ephebate* was the period of obligatory military training for young men aged eighteen to twenty, after which they became full citizens.

Veterans: These men, fifty- to sixty-year-olds, were, like *ephebes*, normally used for territorial guard duty only.

[26] Liberty: It is perhaps instructive to reflect on Plutarch's (and our own) use of the word "liberty" or "freedom." The Battle of Krannonas took place in the summer of 322. It marks the end of Greek resistance to Macedon and the end of the free and independent Greek city-state that had characterized Greek political life from their earliest history.

The British historian, Nicolas Hammond, concludes his *History of Greece* at this point with a discussion of the different uses of freedom and the differing views of Athens' eminent statesmen, Phocion and Demosthenes: "The freedom of the individual may be absolute in the mind or soul, because it is based on self-respect. The freedom of the citizen, which is based on political self-expression, is relative to the needs and rights of other citizens. And the freedom of a state, which is based on self-government, is relative to the needs and rights of other states . . . Historians may rate one form of freedom more highly than the other, in the light of the value they attach to military strength, humane methods, economic prosperity, artistic genius, social justice, or such ideals as pacifism, 'democracy,' or federalism. The statesman is faced by a more immediate and practical task, to preserve the well-being of his state in a world of other states, which requires not only a definition of well-being but also an understanding of other states . . . The Athenian statesmen of 338–322 were not unanimous. Phocion and others believed that the well-being of Athens under the conditions of the time lay in co-operation with the Greek League and Macedon. Demosthenes, Hyperides and others hankered after the earlier form of freedom for Athens, with dominion over others, and they considered that contemporary conditions in the world of states offered a reasonable chance of success. In 323 their calculations proved false. Their cause did not command general support. They misjudged their own strength. Lack of unity at home, weak discipline in the field, dependence on mercenaries, and readiness to admit defeat made them much inferior to the power of Macedon. It is far from certain that Demosthenes has the higher claim to the title of statesman than Phocion in the years from 338 to 322" (Hammond 649-650).

fled the city while Demades, who was unable to pay any part of the fines he owed the city, was granted amnesty and proposed to send **plenipotentiary ambassadors** to Antipater to sue for peace. (Demades had been condemned seven times for proposing measures contrary to the laws of Athens and **had lost his citizen rights,** including the right to address the assembly.) The frightened citizens, not trusting Demades, now summoned Phocion as the only person they trusted in this crisis. "If only you had heeded the advice I gave you in the past," he told them, "we would not now be facing this situation." The assembly then approved Demades' motion and sent Phocion along with others to negotiate the peace with Antipater, who was now camped with his army at Cadmea in Thessaly and preparing to enter Attica. Phocion's first request was that they negotiate the peace before invading Attica. To this, Craterus objected, saying that it was not fair to burden their friends and allies in Thessaly with the provisioning of their large army when they might live off their enemies in Attica. But Antipater, taking him by the right hand, said, "Let us grant Phocion this favor." As for the rest, Antipater told the Athenians he would only offer them the same terms of surrender that Leosthenes had demanded of him when he was shut up in Lamia.

[27] Phocion now returned to Athens to report these terms and then went on to Thebes with the other ambassadors. They brought with them **the philosopher Xenocrates**, whose reputation for virtue and wisdom was so great and far-flung that they believed the mere sight of him would inspire reverence and admiration while preventing violence, cruelty, or anger from arising in the heart of man. Unfortunately, he had the opposite effect on the ignorant and malevolent Antipater, who pointedly ignored Xenocrates while greeting the others. (Later, Xenocrates is reported to have said that Antipater could not bear to look upon the philosopher while secretly plotting such cruelty to the city.) Later, when Xenocrates began to speak, Antipater grew impatient, cut him off, and angrily told him to be quiet. During the ensuing negotiation, he told Phocion that Macedon would make peace with Athens only on the following terms: that the city deliver up Demosthenes and Hyperides; that it adopt **the ancient constitution** making franchise dependent on property ownership; that it accept a Macedonian garrison in Munychia and pay

Fled: In his *Life of Demosthenes*, Plutarch tells us that Demades had obtained a vote from the assembly condemning Demosthenes to death.

Plenipotentiary ambassadors: These are ambassadors granted "full powers" to negotiate on behalf of a city or state that is then obligated, theoretically, to accept whatever terms the ambassadors have agreed upon.

Had lost his citizen rights: as a consequence of being unable to pay his fines.

[27] The philosopher Xenocrates: Xenocrates was a *metic,* a foreign resident, and leader of the Academy from 339. Xenocrates paid the alien-tax in Athens, being a native of Chalcedon across the Bosphorus from Byzantium (later Constantinople, now Istanbul).

The ancient constitution: the constitution as it had existed in the time of Solon and was resurrected briefly by the oligarchies of 411 BC and 404–3 BC.

war reparations and a fine. The other ambassadors accepted these terms as tolerable, all except Xenocrates who said that Antipater's terms would appear lenient to slaves, but to free men, harsh. When Phocion asked that they be spared the garrison, Antipater is said to have replied, "O Phocion, we wish to please you in everything, except in those things that would bring ruin upon ourselves as well as you." Others report instead that Antipater asked if, in exchange for his withdrawing the garrison, Phocion was prepared to give a personal guarantee that Athens would keep the peace and **stop meddling in the affairs of others**. When he hesitated and did not reply at once, Callimedon, **the Lobster**, an arrogant fellow and no friend of democracy, jumped up and said, "If this chap can't give you a straight answer, Antipater, why would you trust him and not go ahead and do as you have proposed?"

[28] And so, the Athenians received a garrison of Macedonians and a governor named Menyllus, a fair-minded man well-disposed toward Phocion. **The imposition of a garrison**, however, was excessive and more a reflection of Antipater's determination to flex his muscles by imposing his will on Athens rather than something warranted by the circumstances. The timing also contributed to a feeling of resentment. The garrison was put in place on the twentieth day of Boedromion during the great festival of the Sacred Mysteries, when the people carry **Iacchos** in procession from the center of the city to Eleusis. When this solemn ritual was disturbed, many began to recall former occasions, both ancient and modern, when portentous signs accompanied these rituals. During the glory years when great victories were being won, **marvelous apparitions and voices** accompanied these ceremonies to shock and terrify their enemies. But now, the gods stood silent witness as they beheld Greece's most wretched suffering and **watched as her most sacred season of joy became profaned and identified with her worst disaster**.

A few years earlier, the prophetesses at Dodona had brought an oracle to Athens, bidding her to protect **the cape of Artemis** lest foreigners should seize it. At this same time, other signs occurred. When they attempted to dye the ribbons with which they wrapped the mystical baskets carried in the procession, the ribbons came out the pale yellow of corpses rather than a vibrant purple. What is more, linens dipped in the same solution kept their original color. Elsewhere, while a candidate for initiation was washing his sacrificial gift, a young pig in **Cantharus harbor**, was seized by a shark which ate its lower parts up to the belly. Obviously,

Stop meddling in the affairs of others: a translation of the very handy Greek word *polypragmosyne*: "busybody-ness." In this context, as in the note on "liberty" above, it points to the limitation of a state's freedom to conduct an independent foreign policy.

The Lobster: an epithet apparently coined by a comic poet. Callimedon was an Athenian who had joined Antipater earlier.

[28] The imposition of a garrison: the ancient equivalent of an army of occupation.

Iacchos: The name given to the god Dionysus (the "god of many names") when he participated in the Eleusinian Mysteries as an attendant of the goddess Demeter. In this context, he was considered to be the son of Zeus and Demeter.

Marvelous apparitions and voices: Plutarch is probably alluding to the apparitions that appeared during this season at the Battle of Salamis, discussed in his Life of Themistocles.

Watched as her most sacred season of joy became profaned and identified with her worst disaster: For Americans, imagine December 7 or 9/11 falling on the fourth of July.

The cape of Artemis: i.e., Munychia, which contained a sanctuary of Artemis.

Cantharus harbor: a small inlet in the Piraeus (*cantharus* means "cup") where, in preparation for being inducted into the mysteries, initiates were expected to wash a young pig.

this was taken to mean that although they had lost the lower part of the city near the sea, they would be able to keep the upper city.

Thanks to Menyllus, the garrison behaved itself and did not oppress the people; however, the new laws deprived over twelve thousand citizens of their rights because they did not own property. Those who remained in the city seemed miserable and suffered every humiliation. On this account, others left the city and moved to Thrace where Antipater provided them with a town and some land, as if they were exiles from a defeated city.

[29] News of the deaths of Demosthenes at Calauria and of Hyperides near Cleones—**recounted elsewhere**—softened the memory of Philip and Alexander and caused the Athenians to wish for the return of those days. In like manner, after the slaying of **Antigonus** and the vicious oppression of those who slew him, a Phrygian farmer was found digging up his land and was asked, "What do you think you're doing?" With a sigh, he responded, "I'm looking for Antigonus." Many found themselves saying much the same thing as they recalled their struggles against those earlier kings who were at least approachable and capable of showing compassion. Not at all like them, Antipater, with his cheap cloak and frugal diet, hypocritically hid his lust for power behind the mask of a common man while treating those under his control with ruthless cruelty.

Nonetheless, Phocion was able to deal with Antipater and saved many from exile by intervening with him. For those who were exiled, he arranged for them not to be removed beyond the **Ceraunian mountains and Tenerus outside of Greece,** but resettled instead in the Peloponnese, where the **sycophant Hagonides** also ended up. He was careful to manage the city's affairs with gentleness and respect for the laws, and he made sure that only men of proven worth and learning held public office. As for the rabble-rousers and busybodies who were wasting away at not being able to address the assembly and stir up trouble, he taught them to be content to stay at home and tend their gardens. And upon seeing Xenocrates paying his foreign residency tax, he offered to register him as a citizen, but Xenocrates refused, saying that he could not accept a franchise the terms of which he had disparaged as an ambassador.

[29] Recounted elsewhere: in Plutarch's Life of Demosthenes.

Antigonus: Antigonus I the One-Eyed was one of Alexander's generals and the Diadoch who most nearly succeeded in reuniting Alexander's empire in a series of Diadochi Wars. He was finally defeated and killed by an alliance between the Diadochs Cassander, Ptolemy, Seleucus, and Lysimachus at the Battle of Ipsus in 301 BC.

Ceraunian mountains and Tenerus outside of Greece: The Ceraunian mountains in Epirus and Cape Tenerus in the southern Peloponnese were considered the northern and southern limits of Greece.

Sycophant Hagnonides: Plutarch's "aside" here is owing to the fact that Hagnonides would be one of Phocion's accusers.

[30] When Menyllus offered him a large gift of money, Phocion declined to accept it by saying that there was no reason to accept from Menyllus what he had refused to accept from Alexander. When Menyllus then urged him to accept the gift for the benefit of his son Phocos, Phocion replied, "If my son adopts a reasonable lifestyle, what he inherits from his father's estate will suffice, but as things now stand, nothing will suffice." But to Antipater, who tried to get him to do some of his dirty work, Phocion responded more rudely, saying, "Antipater cannot have me as both friend and toady." And indeed, Antipater used to say that he had two friends in Athens, Phocion and Demades: the one he could not persuade to accept his gifts, and to the other he could never give enough. It is true that Phocion displayed his poverty as if it were a virtue. He clung to this virtue even as he grew old in spite of having commanded Athens' armies and having kings as friends. Demades, on the other hand, delighted in displaying his wealth even as he made a mockery of the law's intent. For example, there was a law at the time that required a **chorus leader** to pay a fine of a thousand drachmas if he hired a foreigner to appear in his chorus. To show off his fabulous wealth, Demades hired a chorus entirely of foreigners, a hundred of them, and paid the thousand-drachma fine for every one of them. On another occasion, when marrying his son Demeas, he vainly boasted, "Son, when I married your mother, not even our next-door neighbor knew of it, but to your wedding, kings and potentates bring gifts!"

The Athenians kept insisting that Phocion use his influence to convince Antipater to remove the garrison. Whether he had no hope of persuading him or because he saw that the people were behaving reasonably but only kept in line out of fear, he continually put off making this request. Instead, he worked at convincing Antipater to postpone payment of the fine and war reparations owed by the city. And so, frustrated, the people turned to Demades for help. He stepped up eagerly and took his son with him to Macedonia. It must have been his ***daemon*** that arranged it. His timing could not have been worse. Antipater had just come down with a serious illness, and Cassander had taken command. It so happened that Cassander had in his possession a letter that Demades had written to Antigonus in Asia urging him to bring his army to Greece and describing the country as hanging, in a reference to Antipater, "by an old and rotten thread." As soon as he arrived, Cassander had him arrested. Cassander then slit his son's throat right

[30] Chorus leader: The *choregos*, literally chorus leader, roughly corresponds to our producer/ director of a theatrical production. Selected by the archon from among the wealthiest citizens to perform this very visible "public service" (*liturgy* in Greek), he paid the entire production costs while rehearsing and directing the chorus. The intent of the Athenian law seems to have been to reserve for citizens the honor (and employment?) of appearing in the chorus.

Daemon: The ancient Greeks traditionally regarded the divine power that controls an individual's destiny, for good or for ill, as his *daemon*.

in front of him, so close in front that his son's blood splattered all over his clothes and drenched the father in the boy's murder. He then heaped abuse on him for his ingratitude and treachery and, after mocking him, killed him by his own hand.

[31] Having named Polyperchon **strategos** and Cassander **chiliarch**, Antipater died, and Cassander immediately rose up and took charge. Straightaway, he sent Nicanor to take command of the garrison from Menyllus, ordering him to occupy Munychia before the news of Antipater's death reached Athens. A couple days after this was accomplished, the Athenians learned of Antipater's death and angrily blamed Phocion for withholding this information from them. They suspected him of having known this and kept silent about it out of friendship for Nicanor. Phocion brushed this talk aside and made it his duty to meet regularly with Nicanor. Their discussions rendered Nicanor kind and well disposed to the Athenians. Phocion even managed to persuade Nicanor to win the favor of the people by undertaking, at great personal expense, to become an **agonothete**.

[32] At this point Polyperchon, **the king's regent**, tried to undermine Cassander by sending an open letter to **all Athenians**, declaring that the king had decided to restore their democracy and that henceforth they would be governed by their own ancient customs and ancestral laws. **This was all a ruse to put an end to Phocion's influence** as subsequent events showed. Polyperchon wanted to seize control of the city for himself, and he knew that he had no hope of doing this as long as Phocion was on the scene. But he was confident that, as soon as the disenfranchised citizens poured back into the city and the demagogues and sycophants took back control of the assembly, it would not be long before Phocion was driven out.

These prospects set the Athenians all abuzz. Wishing to confer with the people on this subject and entrusting his safety to Phocion, Nicanor attended a meeting of the **Council** in the Piraeus. But there, the commander of the local militia, Dercylus, tried to arrest him. Getting wind of this beforehand, Nicanor made his escape with the clear intention of taking instant revenge on the city for this affront. Phocion was accused of helping him make his getaway by failing to restrain him, and he tried to reassure the people by saying he had complete confidence in Nicanor that he would

[31] *Strategos* . . . *chiliarch*: Polyperchon was named *strategos autocrator* and Cassandra *chiliarch*, literally "leader of a thousand," a title Alexander had adopted from the Persian Empire for the commander of an elite troop of the imperial guard. As noted below in the assumption of Antipater's regency by Polyperchon, the arrangement made Cassander subordinate to Polyperchon, but as Plutarch informs us in [30] this arrangement had been immediately subverted by Cassander.

Agonothete: An *agonothete* sponsored and organized a public contest. The great public contests in Athens were the Panathenaea and the City Dionysia. Both attracted visitors from the rest of the Greek world and involved several days of processions, rituals, and games (in the case of the Panathenaea) or musical and theatrical performances (in the case of the City Dionysia).

[32] **The king's regent**: In his role as *strategos autocrator*, Polyperchon had assumed Antipater's regency of King Philip Arrhidaeus, the feeble-minded son of Philip of Macedon.

All Athenians: i.e., including all those who had lost the franchise due to the property qualification imposed by Antipater.

This was all a ruse to put an end to Phocion's influence: As we might have expected, our other source, Diodorus, tells us that this was part of a general strategy directed at the Greek states in Polyperchon's attempt to undermine Cassander.

Council: The Council had five hundred full time members who prepared the agenda for the Assembly.

not act precipitously or vengefully. "If not," he said. **"I would prefer to suffer an injustice rather than be a party to committing one."**

Although coming from a private citizen, this might sound like a high-minded and noble sentiment, upon reflection, I think it ought to give us pause. Inasmuch as he put his country in danger and uttered it as its leader and general, I wonder if he did not transgress a greater and more sacred form of justice owing his fellow citizens. Nor is it credible to think that Phocion spared Nicanor out of fear that failing to do so would invite a war with Macedon. This is no more credible than saying that he feigned confidence in Nicanor's sense of justice in order to shame him into seeking a peaceful and just resolution with the Athenians. The truth is, Phocion had grown to trust Nicanor without reservation. And in spite of seeing signs and receiving reports that Nicanor was preparing to attack Piraeus—**mercenaries being transported to Salamis and attempts to create a fifth column by bribing the local residents**—Phocion steadfastly refused to pay any attention to these. Even after the assembly passed Philomelus of Lamptrea's proposal that all the Athenians should take up arms and be prepared to follow Phocion, their general sat and did nothing until, at last, Nicanor brought the garrison down from Munychia and encircled the Piraeus with trenches. Finally persuaded that something needed to be done and ready to lead out the Athenians, he found himself jeered and disregarded, without followers.

[33] Meanwhile, Polyperchon's son, Alexander, drew near with his army on the pretext of helping the men of the **town** against Nicanor, but in reality, he wanted to be on hand to take control of the city himself once it collapsed from its own internal divisions and discord. Returning to the city with Alexander were all those who had been previously expelled, and these were joined by a multitude of foreigners and disenfranchised persons. Together, these groups formed an unruly and irregular assembly that stripped Phocion of his office and selected a whole new slate of generals. (Had Alexander not aroused suspicion by being seen from the city walls conversing with Nicanor, not once but repeatedly, the city might not have escaped the trap they were laying.) The orator Hagonides immediately began attacking Phocion and his friends and accusing them of treason. Callimedon, Charicles, and their friends took fright and fled from the city, while Phocion and the friends who stayed with him set out to join Polyperchon.

"I would prefer to suffer an injustice rather than be a party to committing one.": a moral principle articulated in Plato's *Gorgias*.

Mercenaries being transported to Salamis and attempts to create a fifth column by bribing the local residents: Find Salamis on the map below, and consider that, in the long eons of walled cities, the most common way of conquering such a city—barring Trojan horses and catapults—was to bribe or corrupt someone inside the city (a fifth column) to open the gates or foment a revolt.

[33] Town: See the map of Athens below. The ancient town, represented in the insert by the gray area surrounding the acropolis, was joined to the Piraeus by the Long Walls. The base of the Macedonian garrison, Munychia, is visible at the edge of the Piraeus.

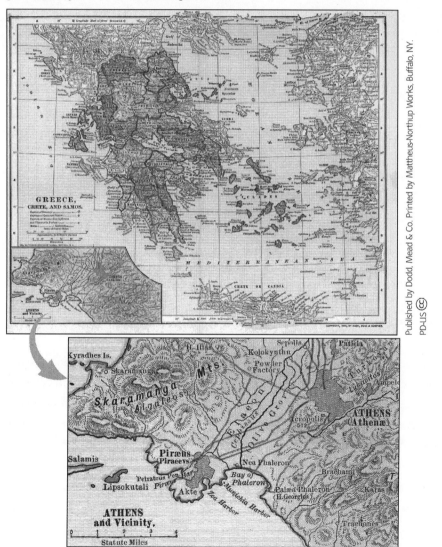

Published by Dodd, Mead & Co. Printed by Mattheus-Northup Works, Buffalo, NY.
PD-US

Out of respect for Phocion, the Plataean Solon and the Corinthian Dinarchus, both considered to be friends of Polyperchon, joined their group. But they were delayed several days in **Elatea** while Dinarchus recovered from an illness, and during this time, on Hagonides' urging and Achestratus' proposal, the assembly in Athens voted to send an embassy to Polyperchon accusing Phocion. Both parties caught up with Polyperchon, who was travelling with the king, outside Pharyges, a village in Phocis now called Galata, at the foot of Mount Acrourion.

On this spot, Polyperchon set up his golden pavilion under which he placed the king and his friends. He promptly arrested Dinarchus, had him tortured, and put him to death. He then invited the Athenians to speak. They all began speaking at once, shouting accusations at one another and making such an uproar that Hagonides stepped forward to say, "Why not shut us all up in a cage and send us back to Athens to have it out in front of the Athenians?" This proposal made the king laugh, and the rest of his company, Macedonians and disinterested foreigners, also found the whole affair quite amusing and urged the delegates to go · on making their case. There was nothing fair about this tribunal. Polyperchon interrupted Phocion whenever he tried to speak until at last he planted his staff in the ground and remained silent. At one point, when Hegemon suggested that Polyperchon himself could attest to Phocion's love for the people, Polyperchon retorted angrily, "Stop slandering me in front of the king!" The king jumped up to run Hegemon through with his spear, but Polyperchon quickly restrained him and dismissed the tribunal.

[34] A guard surrounded Phocion and those with him while those friends of his not close by, seeing what was happening, hid their faces and took flight. Cleitus brought the arrested men to Athens, supposedly to stand trial, but in reality already condemned to die. They were conveyed in open carts and paraded through the Ceramicus and into the theatre where Cleitus held them until the archons could call an assembly of the people. Everyone was invited. They excluded neither slaves nor foreigners nor those whom the new laws had disenfranchised. Men and women alike were welcome to join the court and even sit on the speaker's platform. Before the proceedings began, a letter from the king was read, stating that he knew those being charged were traitors and deserving of death, but that

Elatea: a town in northern Phocis, not far from Thermopylae. Polyperchon had evidently sent his son Alexander ahead with an army and was making his way south with the king.

Athens being a free city, he was handing the judgment over to the people. Cleitus then led the accused in. At the sight of Phocion, the best citizens covered their faces to hide their tears. One man even had the courage to shout out that since the king had entrusted such a serious decision to the people, it would be appropriate for the slaves and foreigners to leave the assembly. But this prompted an angry response from the crowd, shouting that the oligarchs and enemies of the people ought to be thrown out. After this, no one dared to speak in Phocion's defense.

With great difficulty Phocion was eventually heard to ask, "Do you wish to condemn us lawfully or unlawfully?" When the crowd responded "lawfully," he asked again, "How can that be unless you allow us to speak?" When they still refused to listen to him, he stepped forward and said, "I admit my guilt. My mismanagement of the city's affairs is deserving of the death penalty. But why, O men of Athens, do you wish to kill these men who have done nothing wrong?" Many cried out, "Because they are your friends!" Phocion then drew back and said nothing more. Hagonides now came forward and read the decree he was holding and had written out beforehand. It stated simply that by a show of hands the people should vote on whether these men had done wrong and, if so, they should be put to death.

[35] Once the decree was read, some asked that wording be added to the effect that Phocion be tortured and die on the rack. They demanded that the wheel be brought in and the executioners summoned. But Hagonides, seeing that even Cleitus was disgusted and considered the request barbarous and abominable, said, "Men of Athens, when we catch that rascal Callimedon, we will put him on the rack, but as for Phocion, I propose no such thing." At which point one of the more sensible citizens was heard to mutter under his breath, "Quite right, too! If we were to torture Phocion, what would we do to you?!" So the wording of the decree being approved, a show of hands was called for. No one remained seated, and all stood, some with their heads crowned with garlands, and voted to condemn them all. The names of those condemned along with Phocion were Nicocles, Thudippus, Hegemon, Pythocles, **Demetrius of Phaleron**, Callimedon, and Charicles. Others who were absent were condemned to death as well.

[35] **Demetrius of Phaleron:** who would become Cassander's governor in Athens in 317 BC.

[36] So the assembly broke up, and the condemned were led off to prison. Most of them were in tears, surrounded by grieving family and friends and bemoaning their fate, but Phocion—to the astonishment of those observing him—remained as calm and dignified as he did in the days when he returned home from the assembly as a general. His enemies ran alongside him hurling insults. One even came up and spat in his face. Phocion merely turned to the guard and said, "You should stop this poor fellow from disgracing himself." When they reached the prison and saw the **hemlock** being ground, Thudippus broke down and began cursing his bad luck in having to die simply because of his association with Phocion. Hearing this, Phocion commented, "So you are not happy to die with **a friend**?" One of his friends standing by asked him if he had a message for his son **Phocos**, "Yes, please. Tell him not to bear a grudge against the Athenians for this." When Nicocles, his most faithful friend, asked for permission to drink the hemlock first, Phocion said, "O Nicocles, your request causes me great pain, but since in life I was never able to refuse anything you asked, I will not do so now." Everyone then began drinking the poison when it suddenly ran out, and the jailor refused to grind more without being paid twelve drachmas, the cost of another dose. Time dragged on and the poison began working too slowly when Phocion finally asked one of his friends to give the jailor his money, saying, "In Athens we must even pay for the privilege of dying."

[37] This all happened on the nineteenth day in the month of Munychion when it was customary to make a solemn procession in honor of Zeus. As the cavalry escorting this procession passed by, some riders removed their garland crowns while others stopped and wept at the gates of the prison. It was obvious to any citizen not utterly devoid of humanity, whose soul was not steeped in anger and envy, that by not holding off for a day and keeping the city **unsoiled by public execution** on a religious holiday, a great sacrilege was being committed. But so consumed by hatred were his enemies that they felt their triumph was incomplete unless Phocion's corpse be removed from beyond the border and no Athenian be allowed to light his funeral pyre. For this reason, his friends dared not touch his body, and a certain Canopion who was accustomed to do

[36] Hemlock: *Conium* (from the Greek word *kṓneion* meaning hemlock) *maculatum* is the plant that also killed Socrates. In ancient Greece, it was used to poison condemned prisoners. A neuromuscular poison, it paralyzes the muscles beginning, like ALS, in the extremities, and in doses greater than 100 mg causes death due to respiratory failure.

"*A friend*": We have taken an interpretive liberty here. The Greek simply says "Phocion," but in the context of close friends, we wished to emphasize the irony in Phocion's question. What better way to die than in the company of friends?

Phocos: True to what we have learned of his character, Phocion's son is conspicuous in his absence from this scene.

[37] Unsoiled by public execution: a reference to ritual pollution, *miasma* in Greek. The echo with the death of Socrates is already evident, and was no doubt especially poignant to Plutarch as a student of the Academy. Condemned in the anti-elitist democratic reaction of 399 BC, Socrates drank hemlock in this same prison, but his death was delayed in order to await the return of the sacred pilgrimage (*theoria*) to Delos.

Plutarch's account of Phocion's burial inspired two paintings by French artist Nicolas Poussin (1594–1665). **Burial of Phocion** *(above) and* **Landscape with Phocion's Ashes** *(page 70).*

this sort of thing **conveyed the body beyond Eleusis** and burned it using fire from Megara. **Phocion's wife** came with her maidservants and heaped up a hollow mound and poured libations in the place where the body was burned. And gathering up his bones in her lap, she conveyed them by night to their home and buried them near the hearth saying, "To you, *beloved hearth*, I entrust these remains of a good and brave man. Guard and return them, I beg you, to the tombs of his fathers when the Athenians finally come to their senses."

[38] It wasn't long before subsequent events showed the Athenians what a wise counselor and brave defender of justice they had destroyed. They erected a bronze statue of him and buried his bones at the public expense. As for his accusers, Hagonides they voted to execute, and Epicurus and Demophilus fled the city out of fear. His son, Phocos, eventually found and dealt with them. (In other respects, they say, this son was not very respectable. He fell in love with a young girl in a brothel and, having by chance attended a lecture at the Lyceum by the atheist Theodorus, he heard him argue that if ransoming a male friend was a good thing, would not the same logic apply to ransoming a female friend? Making this argument serve his passion for the prostitute, **he decided to purchase her freedom**.) What happened to Phocion reminded the Greeks of what they had done to Socrates, and it became for the city a similar blemish and misfortune.

Conveyed the body beyond Eleusis: The bodies of those condemned for treason were burned in the disputed land between Athens and Megara.

Phocion's wife: A copyist's error in the manuscript gave rise to the misconception that this was not Phocion's wife but instead a woman from Megara.

"Beloved hearth": Hestia, the hearth, focus and protector of the family—and ultimately of the State—was, like the Roman Vesta, worshipped as a goddess.

[38] He decided to purchase her freedom: As a prostitute, she was evidently a slave. The surprised modern reader will agree (we hope) with the son's action and the philosopher Theodorus' reasoning.

Landscape with Phocion's Ashes *by French artist Nicolas Poussin (1594–1665)*

Portrait of Marcus Porcius Cato
Rene Boyvin (1566)

The Life of Cato the Younger

Be Cato's friend, he'll train thee up to great
And virtuous deeds.

–Addison, Cato 2.4

[1] The glorious renown of Cato's family began with **his great–grandfather Cato**, who, owing to his exceptional virtue, became one of ancient Rome's most celebrated and powerful citizens. This I have described in his *Life*.

Cato the Younger, along with his brother, Caepio, and sister, Porcia, was left an orphan. Together with Servilia, Cato's maternal half–sister, the children were all taken in and raised by Livius Drusus, their maternal uncle, a leading statesman at the time. A brilliant speaker and wise counselor, he yielded to no one in dignity and determination.

Even in childhood, Cato is said to have exhibited in his speech, his facial expressions, and all his play an unbending and unflappable character, resolute in all things. In his drive to finish a task, he displayed fortitude far beyond his years. Harsh and dismissive of those who tried to flatter him, he was even rougher on those who dared to threaten him. It was almost impossible to make him laugh; rarely did he even smile. He was not given to anger or easily provoked, but once angered, not soon pacified either.

In his studies, Cato tended to be a slow and indifferent learner, but once he grasped an idea, he never let it go. Indeed, **this seems to be nature's way** of compensating the slow learner. Whereas the gifted student tends to pick up things quickly and subsequently needs to be reminded of them, those who learn with difficulty and after painstaking study remember best. It's as if each painful lesson is branded onto their minds with a hot iron. Cato's natural skepticism and resistance to persuasion may also have made it hard to teach him. Learning, after all, is a matter of accepting a new idea, and it follows that those who are easily convinced are also those least likely to resist a new idea. For this reason, the young are more easily convinced than the old, the sick more than the healthy, and in general those who are in a weakened condition are less likely to raise objections and doubts. In other words, they are more easily persuaded and, hence, taught. They say, however, that Cato obeyed his teacher and followed all his instructions, asking only that he be told the cause and purpose for each lesson. He was indeed fortunate in having an expert teacher, one readier to use reason than the back of his hand. His name was **Sarpedon.**

[1] **His great-grandfather Cato**: generally referred to as Cato the Elder. Marcus Porcius Cato (234–149 BC) had an extensive military and political career and was renowned for his moral conservatism and resistance to Greek influences on Roman life. He is probably most remembered for his hatred of Carthage, expressed at the close of all his speeches in the Senate, regardless of the topic of his speech: "Besides, I believe Carthage ought to be destroyed!" or simply "*Carthago delenda est!*" The bust portrayed below is not of Cato, but it was long believed to be, for reasons not too difficult to guess.

Patrizio Torlonia Torlonia, Patrizio Torlonia PD ©©

The Patrician Torlonia Bust *once thought to be of Cato the Elder*

This seems to be nature's way: Plutarch's remarks in this passage on Cato's education give us an invaluable glimpse of Plutarch the teacher. As a Platonist, he probably viewed knowledge as something that was recollected from within rather than implanted from outside. A slow learner would have difficulty recollecting whereas a gifted student would simply need to be "reminded." This passage also reminds us that the *Parallel Lives* themselves, as well as many of Plutarch's works collected in the *Moralia*, were written with the education of future statesmen in mind.

Sarpedon: a reminder that teachers, like personal secretaries, artists, and craftsmen in the Roman world were more often than not Greek.

[2] When Cato was still a child, **Rome's allies sought to become free citizens of Rome.** A certain **Poppaedius Silo**, a famous man of war, had come to Rome representing the allies to win this favor from the assembly. As a friend of Drusus, he spent several days in their home and became familiar with the children. "Come now," he would say to them, "can't you petition your uncle to fight with us for citizenship rights?" Caepio smiled and nodded his agreement, but Cato refused to say anything and only glared at the foreign guests. Poppaedius then pressed him saying, "So, young man, what have you to say? Are you not able to come to our aid like your brother and put in a good word with your uncle?" Cato said nothing, while by his silence and severe expression showing his refusal. At this point, Poppaedius picked him up as if to throw him out the window. Dangling him from the window by his arms and shaking him several times, he adopted a harsh tone and ordered him to agree or be dropped. After Cato, unfazed and fearless, endured this treatment for some time, Poppaedius finally set him down and said softly to his friends, "How fortunate for Italy that this is just a child. If he were a man I reckon we Italians wouldn't get a single vote in the Roman assembly."

Another time, one of Cato's relatives celebrated a birthday and invited Cato along with some other children to his party. For entertainment, the older and younger children played together on their own in a remote part of the house. They pretended at being magistrates, pleading cases before the court and hauling the guilty off to jail. One of the children "under arrest," an especially beautiful child, was locked in a room by an older boy and called out to Cato for help. Cato, immediately aware of what was happening, ran to the door, shoved aside those who were guarding it, freed the little boy, and angrily led him back to the main house accompanied by the other children.

[3] Cato had already gained a reputation for himself when Sulla instituted the sacred horse race for boys they call **"Troy."** Sulla assembled the sons of the nobility and appointed from their ranks two leaders. One of them the boys accepted since he was the son of Metella, Sulla's wife. But the other, Pompey's nephew Sextus, they rejected, not wishing to train under his command. When Sulla then asked them whom they wished to have lead them, they all shouted "Cato!" and Sextus readily gave way, yielding the honor to Cato as the more worthy.

[2] **Rome's allies sought to become free citizens of Rome**: subsequent to the *Bellum Italicum* (91–88 BC), or War of the Allies (*Bellum Sociale*) as it came to be known. This war was precipitated by legislation, especially the Lex Licinia Mucia of 95 BC, which attempted to purge the citizenship rolls of Latin and Italian allies. The Roman armies were ultimately victorious over their longtime Italian allies; but casualties were heavy on both sides, and the net result was the Romanization of Italy. The map below illustrates the political status of Italy prior to the War of the Allies.

Poppaedius Silo: Quintus Poppaedius Silo belonged to the Marsi, an Italian people living in the mountainous region east of Rome known today as the Abruzzi. Allies of Rome from the end of the fourth century, they provided Rome with some of her most reputable soldiers. It was a march of ten thousand Marsi led by Poppaedius Silo in support of his friend Drusus' pro-Italian legislation in 91 BC and Drusus' subsequent murder that ignited the *Bellum Sociale*. Poppaedius Silo went on to lead the Marsian forces in the war, inflicting heavy losses on the Romans until he was finally defeated and killed by Drusus' brother. The story of young Cato's response that Plutarch tells here adds yet another layer of poignancy to the internecine nature of this conflict. If historical, the incident would have occurred when Cato was three or four years old based on Plutarch's dating (cf. section [73]).

[3] **"Troy"**: The *lusus Troia* or Troy Game is described by Vergil in Book V of the *Aeneid* as the final contest in the funeral games of Anchises. If Sulla did institute the game, as Plutarch says here, it would be the first known historical instance. Otherwise, Suetonius says that Julius Caesar revived the game, and Augustus held it often.

Political Status of the Italian Peninsula
Prior to the Bellum Italicum

It so happened that Sulla was a friend of their family and would sometimes invite Caepio and Cato over to talk with them, a mark of friendship he granted to few owing to the gravity of his office and the extent of his power. Sarpedon attached great importance to these visits for both the honor and the safety it bestowed on his young charges, and he often brought Cato to Sulla's house **to greet him**. At this time, his house looked more like a prison than a home owing to the sheer number of persons being jailed, tortured, and executed there. **Cato was fourteen** at the time. Seeing the heads of some of Rome's most distinguished citizens being carried out and hearing the muffled sighs of those present, Cato asked his tutor, "Why does nobody assassinate this man?" "Because," Sarpedon replied, "they fear him even more than they hate him." "Why then," demanded Cato, "haven't you given me a sword that I might do away with him and free my country from slavery?" Hearing this and seeing the anger and determination in Cato's whole look and bearing, Sarpedon now began to keep a close watch on him, afraid that he might act recklessly and put himself in danger.

When still a small boy and people asked him to name the person he loved most, he would answer, "My brother." And who second? Again, "my brother." And third? Same answer and so on, until the questioner finally gave up asking. As he grew older, his love for his brother only became stronger. By the time he was twenty, he never dined, travelled, or entered the Forum without Caepio. But when Caepio began using myrrh cologne and scenting his body, Cato criticized him for doing so and remained in his own personal habits very plain and austere. In fact, when Caepio was praised for his great temperance and moderation, he allowed that compared to other men he might seem deserving of this praise, "but," he would say, "when compared with Cato, I am no more deserving of praise than Sittius," naming a man notorious for his luxurious and self–indulgent lifestyle.

[4] When Cato entered **the priesthood of Apollo**, he took the inheritance his father had left him, 120 talents, and moved out of the house of Drusus and adopted an even stricter and more disciplined manner of living. Having made friends with Antipater of Tyre, he took to heart this Stoic philosopher's lessons, in particular his moral and political precepts. As if driven by a divine compulsion, he pursued every virtue, but the virtue he most cherished was that of justice, a form of justice that showed neither partiality nor mercy. At this time, he also studied the art of

To greet him: As is often the case in aristocratic societies, the Roman nobleman would spend the early morning hours receiving friends or clients (*clientes*) for whom he was the patron (*patronus*). Plutarch says that this was an integral aspect of Roman society from the time of Romulus.

Cato was fourteen: According to Plutarch's dating, this puts us in 81 BC, the second year of Sulla's dictatorship (82–79 BC).

[4] **The priesthood of Apollo**: Plutarch notes here an honor and role that as a priest at Delphi he shared with Cato. In Roman terms, Cato entered the quindecemvirate (*quindecmviri sacris faciundis*), a college of fifteen men charged with conducting sacrifices and whose duties included guarding and consulting the Sibylline Books, roughly the Roman equivalent of the Delphic Oracle. Cato would have assumed the *toga praetexta*, the purple-bordered toga that protected free-born Roman adolescents, at the age of fourteen. Normally he would not be eligible for the college of quindecemvirs before assuming the *toga virilis* at age seventeen.

The Tyche of Antioch, *a marble copy of a bronze by Eutychides (a name meaning child of Good Fortune) in the Vatican Museum.*

public speaking, believing that just as a great city must have a strong military, the political philosophy of a great city must be articulated forcefully if it were to have any chance of being put into action. But he never practiced his speaking in front of his classmates, and none of them ever heard him speak. When one of his classmates told him, "People criticize your silence, Cato," he responded, "But not my morals, I hope. I will begin to speak when there is more value in what I have to say than in silence."

[5] The so–called **Basilica Porcia** was built and dedicated for public use during the censorship of the Elder Cato. It was here that the plebian tribunes conducted their business. Because they complained that one of the hall's columns blocked their seating arrangements, they debated whether to move it or tear it down. This is what first compelled Cato, much against his will, to enter the Forum. He opposed the tribunes, and his courage and eloquence on this occasion caused quite a sensation. His speech was neither juvenile nor ornate, but instead straightforward, substantive, and harsh. Yet there was a certain grace that accompanied the roughness of his speech and put on full display the strength of the speaker's character and grabbed the attention of his listeners and pleased them. His voice—powerful, vigorous, and indefatigable—was loud enough to be heard by everyone in the large assembly. Indeed, he was subsequently often called upon to speak for an entire day in public.

On this occasion, however, he won his case and resumed his quiet life. He also trained his body with hard work and strenuous exercise, and he made a habit of going bareheaded in both the extreme heat of summer and the bitter cold of winter. In all seasons and at all hours, he walked rather than rode. When he traveled with friends, they on horseback, he on foot, he would come alongside one of them and then another, conversing with them as he walked beside them. In illness, he showed remarkable endurance and self–control; and when he suffered from a fever, he isolated himself and refused to see anyone until the fever had passed.

[5] **Basilica Porcia**: The Basilica Porcia was built on the order of Cato the Elder in 186 BC. Deriving its name from a Greek term for a royal tribunal, it was a large rectangular building principally used for public trials with a dais for magistrates at the far end. Situated in the old Roman Forum, the Basilica Porcia was the first such basilica built, and it would be imitated in towns throughout the Roman world, eventually giving its name to the architectural form of Christian churches. The Basilica Porcia was destroyed in 52 BC by a fire started in the adjoining Curia.

Cato *by Pietro Perugio (created between 1497 and 1500)*

[6] At banquets, a throw of dice decided the choice of dishes. If Cato was unlucky and his friends nevertheless offered him his choice, he would decline their offer saying it wasn't wise to go against the wishes of **Venus**. At first, he would only have a drink after supper and then walk home, but as time went on, he drank much more, often continuing to drink wine until dawn. His friends excused him for this by saying that having spent all day on politics and public business, he was deprived of intelligent conversation and needed to spend his nights **discussing philosophy over drinks.** When a certain Memmius was heard to accuse Cato of spending whole nights drinking, Cicero responded by asking, "Why not also accuse him of spending his days gambling?" But in general, Cato was so much at odds with the manners and mores of his time that he tried whenever possible to oppose them. For example, when he noticed that the lightest and brightest shade of **purple** was then in fashion, he made sure his toga was almost black. He would often go out after breakfast to conduct business barefoot and without his tunic. In this novelty, he wasn't looking for notoriety, but wanted instead to accustom himself to be ashamed of those things that are truly shameful rather than those things that shock popular opinion. When his cousin by the same name (Cato) died and left him an inheritance of one hundred talents, he converted it to silver and kept it on hand and offered to lend it without interest to any friend in need. And he even allowed some friends to use his property and slaves as collateral to secure loans from the public treasury.

[7] When he thought it was time to marry, having never had sexual relations with a woman, he proposed to Lepida, who had previously been engaged to **Scipio Metellus** but was free at the time, having been rejected and their engagement broken off by Scipio. Before the marriage, however, Scipio changed his mind and did everything he could to win the girl back. In this, he succeeded. Cato, fit to be tied and in a violent rage, resolved to take him to court, but his friends persuaded him against it. Instead, he vented his spleen by showering Scipio with angry iambic verse in the bitter, sarcastic style of **Archilochus**, but without descending into puerile obscenities. After this he married Atilia, the daughter of Serranus, the first but not the only woman he ever knew. **More fortunate** was Laelius, Scipio's friend, who in the many years he lived knew only a single woman, the one he married.

[6] **Venus**: Venus was the name given the highest throw of the dice. A person selected by this lucky throw to preside at a banquet or drinking party was said to have been selected by Venus. Compare Horace, *Odes* ii.7.

Discussing philosophy over drinks: It was the custom of aristocratic men to gather after dinner for a *symposium*, literally a drinking party, at which they would be entertained by philosophers, poets, musicians, et al. or entertain one another with discussion, from time to time having a slave fill their cups from a crater of diluted wine. Plato's *Symposium* gives us a delightful glimpse into just how entertaining such discussion could be and, in the end, how open to drop-in guests.

Purple: The purple-bordered *toga praetexta*, in addition to being worn by free-born adolescents, was the public dress of *curule* magistrates and certain priesthoods.

[7] **Scipio Metellus**: Scipio Metellus will play an important role in the closing chapters of this *Life*, when the anecdote recorded here takes on renewed significance.

Archilochus: Generally acknowledged to be the earliest surviving Greek lyric poet from the seventh century BC, Archilochus became a byword in antiquity for hard-hitting invective written in iambic meter even if his poetry is not limited to invective and his invective not limited to iambs.

More fortunate: Plutarch's attitude toward sexuality and chastity as revealed in this passage seems to indicate a sensibility that would be reinforced in late antiquity.

[8] When **the slave war** broke out, the one they call the war with Spartacus, Gellius was in command, and Cato joined the army as a volunteer in solidarity with his brother Caepio, who was a military tribune. The incompetence of those in command denied Cato the opportunity to demonstrate his valor and courage in combat; however, compared with the lax and craven behavior of his comrades in arms, he proved to be the model of discipline, courage, and boldness in all his encounters with the enemy. His military intelligence appeared in no way inferior to that of the Elder Cato. Gellius wrote him up for extreme valor and outstanding honors, but Cato refused them all, saying that he had done nothing to deserve them. For this reason he was regarded as odd and eccentric.

There was a law passed at about this time making it unlawful for candidates for office to use **nomenclators**. When Cato later sought a **military tribuneship**, he was the only candidate to obey this law. He studied to perform this task himself and was able to greet and address all of those he canvassed by name. This caused great discomfort even among those who praised him for it. While recognizing the nobility and impressiveness of his achievement, they were also oppressed—and perhaps made not a little envious—by the thought of how difficult it would be to follow his example.

[9] On being named military tribune, Cato was sent into Macedonia to serve under **the praetor Rubrius**. His wife was much distressed and in tears over this news, and wishing to comfort and reassure her, his friend Munatius said, "Take heart, Atilia. I'll watch over him for you." Cato readily acceded to this offer, saying, "Absolutely!" And, after only the first day's march, following dinner, Cato turned to Munatius and said, "Come now, Munatius, to be sure you keep your promise to Atilia, you must never leave me, day or night." From that moment on, he ordered that their two beds be placed in the same room, and he teased Munatius, saying that Cato was now watching over him. In all, **fifteen house slaves accompanied him, two freedmen**, and four friends traveling by horse. As was his custom, he walked beside his friends, talking to each in turn.

When they arrived in camp, the praetor gave him command of one of the several legions there. He did not begin his command by parading his achievements since, as we have said, he regarded any marks or evidence of his **honor as personal possessions and any boast or display of them as ignoble.** Rather, he set

[8] **The slave war**: known as the Third Servile War (73–71 BC) or War of Spartacus, the slave commander. The first two major slave uprisings had occurred in Sicily, which after the defeat of Carthage in the Punic Wars had become Rome's breadbasket, containing vast estates worked by "armies" of slaves. The size of the slave army in the First Servile War (135–132 BC):– figures vary from seventy thousand to two hundred thousand:—and the number of slave prisoners crucified by the Romans at the war's conclusion, twenty thousand, give some indication of the plantation system in place. It was not unusual, we are told, for a single estate to be worked by four thousand slaves. The Second Servile War (104–101 BC) was on a somewhat smaller scale but took even longer to put down and ended dramatically with the prisoners who had been led to Rome to hunt in a gladiatorial game killing themselves quietly with their swords instead. This final Servile War began in Italy's fashionable heartland with the escape from Capua of seventy gladiators led by Spartacus. They were eventually joined by one hundred and twenty thousand escaped slaves and gladiators and ravaged the Italian countryside for the better part of two years, defeating praetorian and consular armies, until legions under the command of Crassus, and reinforcements under Pompey and Lucullus were sent against them. They were finally defeated in a pitched battle by Crassus. Altogether eleven thousand prisoners were crucified by Crassus and Pompey along the Appian Way. This conclusion led to a tentative alliance between Crassus and Pompey and their joint election to the consulships of 70 BC, this despite the fact that Pompey at thirty-five was underage, an *equis,* and therefore not of senatorial rank and had never held an elected office in the *cursus honorum,* the accepted order of magistracies on the way up to a consulship.

Nomenclators: *Nomenclatores* usually attended candidates for office and reminded them of the names of those they were canvassing (also a common practice in American politics). Knowing the names of their fellow citizens was a decisive skill in Roman politics. What is described by Plutarch as having been in this case performed by Cato himself was normally performed by a slave. The evidence suggests that Cato used nomenclators in later elections.

Military tribuneship: A military tribuneship was a preliminary step before embarking on the *cursus honorum,* the (much more regimented) Roman equivalent of our "political ladder". Military tribunes served as staff officers in the Roman army.

[9] **The praetor Rubrius**: Marcus Rubrius commanded the legions in Macedonia as propraetor in 67 BC. "Praetor" was the original Latin word for a commander or general, and it still carried that meaning after the praetors' role in Rome had evolved into a judicial one. The Senate normally assigned imperial duties (generalships or governorships, which were rarely mutually exclusive) to the praetors and consuls in the year following their year of service, designating them propraetors and proconsuls.

Fifteen house slaves accompanied him, two freedmen: Our readers might remember Phocion's wife's one maidservant at this point. For the Roman aristocrat, a train of seventeen servants is extremely modest.

Honor . . . ignoble: We have translated Plutarch's *arête* as "honor" in this context, and his *ou basilikon* (not royal) as "ignoble." The latter has caused some editors of the Greek text to substitute a word more appropriate to a Roman republican, for whom "royal" seems out of place. Plutarch, being a Greek, uses the term elsewhere without the negative connotations one expects from a Roman.

out with the intention of making those he led similar to himself, not by removing their fear of his authority but by helping them to understand the reasons for it. Because he used his authority to persuade and teach on every occasion, when the time came to reward or punish, his men accepted his decisions, and it was difficult to say whether they were becoming more peace–loving or warlike, more eager to give battle or to see justice done. In this way, they appeared more terrible to their enemies and more kind to their allies, more afraid to do wrong and more eager to win praise. What Cato sought least is what he received in full measure: glory, admiration, approbation, and the affection of his soldiers. What he expected from his troops, he did himself. In his dress, his diet, and his habit of traveling by foot, he more resembled his men than their officers. Yet in his character, his intelligence, and his eloquence, he surpassed even those one salutes as **supreme commanders** and generals, and by these qualities, he earned the admiration and love of his men. To be sure, only admiration and love for the virtuous man can produce in others a true love of virtue. Those who praise good men without loving them may respect their reputation, but they will not imitate their virtue.

[10] While serving with the army, Cato learned that Athenodorus, also called Cordylion, a renowned practitioner of Stoic philosophy, was staying in Pergamum. Already an old man, this philosopher had steadily refused and fought off any acquaintance or association with commanders and kings. Knowing this, Cato reckoned that there would be no point in writing or sending a messenger to him, and since by law, he had a two–month leave coming from the army, he decided to sail to Asia Minor to see the man himself, trusting in his own abilities not to be unlucky in the hunt to win over the old philosopher. As it happened, he was right and was able to convince Athenodorus to return with him to the camp. He came back to camp, overjoyed and bursting with pride, as if he had achieved a conquest more heroic and glorious than any of those that **Pompey and Lucullus were at that time achieving**.

[11] When he was still in the army, his brother, on his way to Asia, fell ill at Aenos in Thrace. A letter informing Cato of this was immediately sent to him, but there was a great storm at sea at this time, and Cato was not able to act upon the news because there was no vessel of sufficient size available to hazard these

Supreme commanders: Plutarch uses the term *autokrator* here, the word that would, like *imperator* in Latin, become the title of the Roman emperors from Augustus on. The transition from Late Republic to Empire could in part be characterized by the shift from rival *autokratores* to a single *autokrator*. Noteworthy, too, is the difference between the Greek and Latin titles: the Greek word evolved from meaning "one's own master" to meaning "absolute ruler" whereas the Latin meant "commander" or simply "the one who gives orders."

[10] **Pompey and Lucullus were at that time achieving**: At that time Pompey had cleared the Mediterranean of pirates with remarkable speed and taken over Lucullus' command of the Third Mithradatic War in the Pontus. In the few years that followed, Pompey would go on to conquer and reorganize the Caucasus, Syria, and Judea: in short, the whole of Roman Asia.

conditions. Eventually, Cato and two of his friends, along with three slaves, set sail from Thessalonica in a small merchant ship. Their boat very nearly capsized, and they narrowly escaped drowning before arriving in Aenos just as Caepio died. Cato bore this loss more like a loving brother than a sober philosopher, not only in his sobbing and embracing of the dead body, but also in his lavish outlay and arrangements for the funeral, in the costly perfumes and expensive garments burned with the corpse, and in the massive monument of Thracian marble, costing eight talents and erected in Aenos' marketplace. There were some, of course, who carped about this, contrasting it with his usual composure and frugality and not realizing how a man so indifferent to pleasures, untouched by fears, and unyielding to unreasonable requests can also show great kindness and tender affection. Both cities and rulers sent him many gifts to honor his dead brother, but he accepted only incense and ornaments, never money, and he repaid the senders the cost of their gifts. And later, when dividing up Caepio's inheritance between himself and his brother's daughter, he paid all the funeral expenses out of his portion of the inheritance. Yet, in spite of all he had done and was doing, there was **one man who wrote** that he sifted through his brother's ashes with a sieve in order to retrieve the gold that was melted down when the body was burnt. This man must have believed that neither his pen nor his sword would ever be questioned or held accountable.

[12] When Cato's military service came to an end, he was sent off not only with blessings and commendations, as was common, but with tears and endless embraces. His soldiers laid down their cloaks for him to walk on and kissed his hands as he passed, honors that the Romans at that time rarely bestowed on even their supreme commanders. Before returning to political life, Cato wanted **to travel and learn about** Asia, to observe the customs, manner of living, and strength of each province. At the same time he did not want to refuse the hospitality of **Deiotorus of Galatia**, an old and dear friend of his father's, who was eager for him to visit. This is how he organized his trip. A day in advance, he would send his baker and his cook to the place where he intended to stay the next night. They would enter the town very quietly and discretely, and if there happened to be no friend or acquaintance of Cato or his family there, they would prepare his reception at a local inn without disturbing anybody. If there were

[11] **One man who wrote**: Plutarch is referring to Caesar. After Cato's suicide in 46 BC, a propaganda battle ensued. Cicero wrote a tract against Caesar entitled *Cato*, to which Caesar responded with his *Anticatones*. Neither work survives except in fragments.

[12] **To travel and learn about**: Plutarch's phrase, more literally "to travel around by way of research," recalls the opening (and title) of Herodotus's *Histories*: "Of Herodotus of Halicarnassus the exposition of his research (*historia*) is as follows."

Deiotorus of Galatia: This tetrarch and king of Galatia was remarkably successful in navigating his alliance with Rome throughout the period, deftly befriending in succession Pompey, the Republicans, Caesar, and Mark Antony, as the fortunes of these bitter rivals shifted.

no inn available, then and only then would they ask the local authorities to help them find lodging. Whatever hospitality the authorities provided, they gratefully accepted. But because his servants made their requests without bragging or making a big fuss, the authorities often slighted or ignored them. Consequently, many times Cato would arrive and find that no arrangements for his stay had been made. At this point, the situation became even worse as those who passed by, seeing him sitting in silence on his luggage, assumed that he was some beggarly poor fellow of no consequence, afraid to make any demands on their hospitality. When things had finally reached this stage, Cato was in the habit of summoning the local authorities and lecturing them thus: "You fools, as if your lack of hospitality is not damning enough, consider this: Not all your visitors will be Catos. The world is full of powerful men who would like nothing more than to take from you by force what you have failed to give freely."

[13] While traveling in this manner, something amusing happened to him in Syria. As he approached Antioch, he noticed outside the city gates a great crowd of people lined up on either side of the road. These included a group of **ephebes** in uniform on one side and many smartly dressed children on the other. Also in the crowd were priests and magistrates in immaculate garments wearing crowns. Cato, thinking all of this was for him, the city's way of honoring and welcoming him, became angry with the friends accompanying him for arranging this reception, and he ordered them to dismount and walk beside him. As they approached the gates of the city, an elderly man who appeared to be in charge, staff in hand and wearing a crown, came up to Cato without greeting him and asked him where he had left Demetrius and at what hour they could expect him. (**This Demetrius was the servant of Pompey, on whom the eyes of the whole world, so to speak, were fixed at this time. On account of his assumed influence with his master, he was accorded great deference and respect.**) Cato's friends fell to laughing so hard that they couldn't stop as they passed through the crowd, while Cato, downright discombobulated, could only mutter, "O what an ill–starred town!" and was otherwise speechless. Later, however, whether telling the story himself or being reminded of it, he was able to laugh about it.

[13] **Ephebes**: As noted earlier in the *Life of Phocion*, these were young men undergoing military training, roughly the equivalent of cadets.

(This Demetrius was the servant of Pompey, on whom the eyes of the whole world, so to speak, were fixed at this time. On account of his assumed influence with his master, he was accorded great deference and respect.): On Pompey's position in the East at this time, and in the entire Roman world for that matter, see our note above. The word Plutarch uses for Demetrius here normally designates a house slave, but in his *Life of Pompey* he calls him a freedman, which is more likely at this point.

[14] Pompey himself, however, set those straight who, through ignorance, failed to honor Cato. When Cato finally arrived at Ephesus and went to pay his respects to Pompey, who was his senior and as supreme commander of Rome's legions the more famous of the two, Pompey sprang from his chair as soon as he saw him, as one would to greet a superior, and taking him by the hand, he made a great show of his affection. Whether to his face or behind his back, Pompey spoke only praise of Cato's virtues, to such an extent that everyone now turned their attentions to him, admiring in him those very qualities they had once criticized, his calm temperament and high–mindedness.

At the same time, it did not escape notice that Pompey seemed more interested in cultivating than in befriending him. He made much of him when he was present but was also happy to see him leave. When other young men came to see him, he typically urged them to stay, but, as if fearful of being found wanting in Cato's eyes, he never held him back and always sent him off gladly. Yet of all those who made their way back to Rome, it was only Cato to whom he entrusted his children and his wife, who was also related to him.

After this, all the cities through which Cato passed tried to outdo one another in honoring him with invitations and feasts. On account of this, he asked his friends to keep a strict watch on himself lest he turn into the kind of Roman his friend Curio, who disliked Cato's rough manners and austere temperament, predicted that he might become when he asked if he was looking forward to his travels through Asia after leaving the army. When Cato responded by saying, "Very much so," Curio said, "Delighted to hear it! Maybe you'll acquire more graceful manners and a more gentle disposition." **That is roughly the wording he used.**

[15] **Deiotarus of Galatia, now a very old man**, sent for Cato, wishing to commend his children and household to him for his protection. When he arrived, he showered him with all sorts of presents, trying by every means to win him over. This really annoyed Cato, so much so that he spent only one night with him and left **at the third hour** the next day. But he had not gone more than a day's journey when he found waiting for him in Pessinous even more gifts along with a letter from Deiotarus begging him to accept them or, failing that, to allow his friends to have them since Cato's own personal resources would not allow

[14] **That is roughly the wording he used**: Plutarch is evidently translating from the Latin. For the Romans, Hellenized Asia was renowned for its cultural wealth and refinement. We have here a classic example of the conflict of Roman attitudes to Greek culture and the fidelity of Cato the Younger to the Elder Cato's famed mistrust of Greek influence on Roman manners.

[15] **Deiotarus of Galatia, now a very old man**: On Deiotarus, see the note above. Deiotarus would go on to live and reign in Galatia until 40 BC.

At the third hour: meaning the third hour after sunrise, the daytime being divided into twelve hours.

him to reward them as friends of his deserved. But Cato would hear none of it, even though he saw that some of his friends were more than willing to accept the gifts and thought he was being too severe and inflexible. "One can always find a pretext for accepting bribes," he told them, "and as my friends, you will always share in whatever I come by honestly and justly." Having said this, he sent Deiotarus' gifts back to him.

Before setting sail for **Brundisium**, Cato's friends tried to persuade him to put his brother's ashes in another ship. But he said he would rather part with his own life than be separated from Caepio's remains. As it happened, Cato only narrowly escaped shipwreck on **the crossing** while others crossed at this time tolerably well.

[16] Once back in Rome, Cato spent his time either at home talking with Athenodorus or in the forum helping his friends. Although he was now of an age when he was eligible to become a **quaestor**, he did not pursue the post until after he had studied the laws governing the Treasury and learned from persons of experience everything pertaining to the powers and responsibilities of the position. Armed with this knowledge, once he assumed the office, he undertook a wholesale reform of the officers and clerks of the Treasury. These were men with extensive experience in handling and maintaining the public records and accounts in accordance with the laws. It was only natural, then, that these men were not willing to submit to the authority of young, inexperienced quaestors who obviously needed instruction. That is, until Cato vigorously took charge, not as a figurehead and magistrate in name only, but as someone with a thorough knowledge of the business and with every intention of exercising the full authority of his office. He treated the officers and clerks like the public servants they were while exposing the corrupt and instructing the ignorant. The more brazen officers tried to oppose him by flattering the other quaestors and trying to turn them against him. But Cato acted quickly, accusing the ringleader of committing fraud in the case of an inheritance and dismissing him from the Treasury. A second he charged with willful negligence and brought him to trial. The censor Lutatius Catulus came forward to defend him. Now, this was a serious matter since Catulus was held in high esteem, not only owing to his office and his reputation for virtue, but because of the general belief that he surpassed all Romans of his time in

Brundisium: modern day Brindisi on the heel of Italy. This was the termination point of the Appian Way, the road built by the Roman legions leading out of Rome to the East, and the embarkation point for ships coming from and going to the East.

The crossing: Until well into the modern era, leaving the coast of the Mediterranean and taking to the open sea—as was necessary in this case to cross the Adriatic from Greece to Brindisi— was a hazardous affair and generally avoided during the winter months (See F. Braudel I, 301 ff.). It appears from Plutarch's account that travelling with his brother's remains was considered unlucky.

[16] **Quaestor**: The post of quaestor was the first official step in the *cursus honorum* open to men of patrician families at the age of thirty and plebeian families at the age of thirty-two. Those who held the office became senators at that point. Cato served as quaestor in either 65 or 64 BC, most likely the latter.

wisdom and justice. Moreover, he was a good friend of Cato's and a great admirer of his manner of living. Seeing that, based on the merits of the case, he was bound to lose, Lutatius openly pleaded for a pardon. But Cato wouldn't allow it. When Lutatius persisted in pressing for a pardon, Cato said, "How can you allow these our servants, Catulus, to corrupt our city, you whose job it is as censor to uphold the law and make sure our citizens do the same!" Hearing this, Catulus looked at Cato as if to respond but said nothing. Whether out of anger or from shame, he left the courtroom deeply agitated and in silence.

The man, nevertheless, was not convicted. The votes for acquittal outnumbered those for conviction by one. This came about as follows: since Marcus Lollius, Cato's colleague in the quaestorship, was ill and absent at the trial, Catulus sent for him, asking that he vote in favor of the defendant. He was conveyed to the place in a litter and placed his vote for acquittal. From that day forward, Cato never made use of this clerk, took away his pay, and refused to acknowledge Lollius' vote.

[17] Having put the officers and clerks of the Treasury in their place, Cato wasted no time in making the Treasury more respectable than the Senate so that everyone both said and thought that, thanks to Cato, the office of quaestor was now as prestigious as that of consul. To begin with, he discovered that there were many who owed old debts to the Treasury as well as many others whom the Treasury owed. He put a stop at once to these wrongs done to and by the State. He demanded exact and immediate payment from those who owed money, and he paid out quickly and graciously to those whom the State owed. And the people rejoiced—and were not a little amazed—to see those paying in full what they thought they could steal from the public purse while others received what they had never hoped to get back.

Next, since many title claims were recorded incorrectly, and there were many dubious judgments based on pretended orders of the Senate or special favors, Cato cast a skeptical eye on all of this. One day, for example, he had doubts about the validity of a judgment, and, even after several persons bore witness to it, he distrusted it and refused to pay it until the consuls also swore to it.

There were, at this time, a great many men whom Sulla had given a bounty of twelve thousand drachmas apiece for killing those on his **proscription** list.

[17] **Proscription:** From a word previously used for posting items for sale, proscription became a particularly ugly feature of the Late Republic. Sulla, in 82–81 BC and then again the Second Triumvirate (Antony, Lepidus, and Octavian) in 43–42 BC posted lists of their political enemies, declaring them outlaws whose property was confiscated and whose sons and grandsons were forbidden from becoming senators. Their pretext was revenge for the massacres of Marius and the assassination of Caesar respectively, but their purpose was to get rid of political enemies, create vacancies for friends, accumulate wealth, and obtain land for veterans.

Everyone hated these accursed and bloodstained men, but no one dared touch them. Cato charged each one of them with illegally receiving public monies and ordered them to repay the Treasury in full, all the time while using language that shamed and abused them for their unlawful and unholy deeds. No sooner were they found guilty of taking money from the State then they were held liable for murder. Guilt of the one proved the other. They were brought before the judges and paid the penalty for their crimes. The people rejoiced. Finally, it seemed that the tyranny of the times was now abolished and Sulla himself punished.

[18] What most impressed the people was Cato's untiring diligence and dedication to his work. He was the first quaestor to arrive at the Treasury and the last to leave. Nor did he ever miss an assembly or meeting of the Senate. He was ever on guard against those who would use their office to do personal favors, to forgive someone's taxes, or to make a grant to someone else. By keeping the Treasury honest, cleansed of toadies, and filled with money, he demonstrated that the city could grow rich without robbing its citizens. Although at first his colleagues regarded him as severe and heavy–handed, they were later delighted with the way he gave them a perfect excuse for refusing to gratify their friends' requests for special favors and grants of public monies. "Sorry, can't do it. Cato won't allow it."

On his last day as quaestor, almost the whole city showed up to accompany him home. Before he reached his house, however, word arrived that Marcellus, surrounded by a group of influential and powerful acquaintances, was being pressured to forgive a debt this group owed and make it appear instead as a gift from the State. Marcellus was a childhood friend of Cato's and his best colleague in the Treasury, but, left on his own, was easily influenced by lobbyists and wanted only to please others. Cato immediately turned around and headed back to the Treasury. Seeing that Marcellus had already registered the amounts they were demanding, he lay hold of the tablets and struck out the amounts with Marcellus standing by in silence. Having done this, he led Marcellus out of the Treasury and walked home with him. Not then or at any later time did Marcellus blame him, but he remained ever afterwards his close friend.

Even after Cato ceased to be quaestor, he kept a watchful eye on the Treasury. His servants he expected to keep an up–to–date record of every day's financial transactions, and he purchased for **five talents** and at his own expense the scrolls

[18] **Five talents:** This detail gives us a nice glimpse into the cost of having these records copied.

that contained the accounts of the Treasury from the time of Sulla until his own quaestorship. These he always kept close at hand.

[19] He was also the first to enter the Senate and the last to leave. Often as the other Senators casually gathered, he would sit apart from them quietly reading with his toga in front of **his book**. He never traveled when the Senate was in session. When later, Pompey and his followers saw how steadfastly Cato opposed their unjust legislation, they contrived to draw him away from the Senate to plead the case of friends in court, or arbitrate their differences, or help them in other business. Cato quickly saw through their scheme and defeated it by telling his friends no longer to call on him for assistance when the Senate was in session. Unlike many others, Cato was not drawn to public life hoping to become rich or famous, nor did he fall into it for lack of anything better to do. He chose politics as the proper job for a good man. His obligations to the commonweal, he believed, should be no less than the bee's to its hive. Accordingly, he asked that his Roman and foreign friends in every province of the empire send him news of all local decrees, legal decisions, and important acts.

One day, he confronted the notorious demagogue, **Clodius**, who was beginning to stir up trouble and promote violent revolution in the assembly by slandering some of the priests and priestesses, among them Fabia, the sister of Terentia, Cicero's wife. He heaped **opprobrium** on Clodius and forced him to leave the city. When Cicero later thanked him, he replied simply, "You should thank the city and not me, for it is my obligations to the city that inspire whatever I do as a politician." This incident so enhanced his reputation that, on a later occasion, the court was heard to reprimand a lawyer for producing only a single witness by telling him, **"It's not right to bring only a single witness before the court,** even if it were Cato himself!" It became a kind of saying among the Romans that if anyone made an incredible claim or assertion, they would respond, "I wouldn't believe that even if Cato himself swore to it!" When a dissolute and shameless spendthrift was haranguing the Senate about the need for more moderation and economy, Amnaeus finally cut him off saying, "Do we really need to endure the babbling of a man who dines with Crassus, builds like Lucullus, and then counsels like Cato?" So, generally speaking, people made fun of those who made a show of speaking with grave earnestness while leading undisciplined and reckless lives by calling them **Pseudo-Catos.**

[19] **His book**: This anecdote is found in Cicero's *de finibus* 3.2.7 where he also says that he would find Cato sitting in a library in Tusculanum surrounded by books by the Stoics. Valerius Maximus, in his *Facta et Dicta Memorabilia* 8.7, adds that the books he read in the Curia would be Greek, not surprising given his penchant for the Stoics.

Clodius: Here we get our first glimpse of Publius Clodius Pulcher, whom Latin students will know from Cicero's unsuccessful defense of his rival Milo in the affair of his murder, the *Pro Milone* in 52 BC, and for the popular identification of Catullus' Lesbia with his sister, Clodia Pulchra. Clodius' troublemaking heydays seem to have begun after the Catalinarian conspiracy in 63 with the *bona dea* scandal in 62 BC, when he was caught dressed as a woman attending the Good Goddess' sacred rites supervised by the Vestal Virgins and hosted by the Pontifex Maximus Caesar's wife Pompeia in an apparent attempt to seduce her. He became a bitter enemy of Cicero and of Cato, and his street gangs would play a disruptive role in the shifting power struggles between Pompey, Crassus, and Caesar in the period popularly known as the First Triumvirate (60—53 BC). Plutarch's narrative appears to be chronological at this point, however, and Clodius did leave Rome in 64 to join the military staff of Lucius Murena in Gaul before returning to Rome in 63 BC.

Opprobrium: From the Latin *ob* (against or in the face of) plus *probrum* (a shameful or vile deed) and defined as "public disgrace arising from shameful conduct." This word is used less frequently today than it used to be but seems particularly fitting in this context.

"**It's not right to bring only a single witness before the court**": The *Lex Acilia* of 123 BC limited the number of witnesses to forty–eight, but there was no required minimum (Chroust and Murphy, 26f.). The defending lawyer here is simply implying the obvious weakness of the accusation.

Pseudo–Catos: This is the term Cicero uses once in a letter to Atticus. One editor amended the Greek text in this sense even if Plutarch's meaning is clear enough as it stands, an instance of Roman sarcasm.

[20] There were many who wanted him to continue in public office and seek the **plebian tribuneship**, but Cato demurred, thinking that the power of so great an office, like a strong medicine, was only needed in the direst of circumstances. At this time, there seemed no need for this in Rome, and Cato seized the opportunity to enjoy a **not illiberal** holiday by taking his books and philosopher friends with him to **Lucania** where he owned a country estate. On the way, he encountered a great number of pack animals with luggage and slaves from whom he learned that Metellus Nepos was making his way to Rome and preparing to stand for the tribuneship. This stunning bit of news froze him on the spot, and, after some hesitation, he ordered his train to turn around and return to Rome. When his friends expressed their surprise, he said, "Don't you understand how greatly to be feared is the stupidity of Metellus? As the tool of Pompey, he will fall upon the state like a hurricane and plunge it in ruin. This is no time to be on holiday or on the road. We must either defeat this fellow or die nobly fighting in defense of our liberty." Nevertheless, on the advice of his friends, he did go first to his country estate and spent a short time there before returning to Rome. Arriving in the evening, the very next morning he made straight for the Forum where he began campaigning for the tribuneship in opposition to Metellus. (The importance of this office lies in its power to oppose rather than to act. Even if every tribune save one votes to approve a measure, that one no vote kills the whole measure.)

[21] At first, only a few friends supported him, but once his intentions were known, every decent and distinguished citizen rushed to his side to support and encourage him. It wasn't as if he were asking them to do him a favor. Rather, it was clear that he was offering to render a great service to his country and its most reasonable citizens. In the past, he had no interest in holding an office that accomplished nothing, but **now, at considerable risk to himself, he entered the arena to fight for the free republic**. It is said that the people's zeal and love for him was so great that he was almost crushed by the thronging crowd as he made his way to the Forum.

He was chosen tribune along with others, including Metellus, and seeing that votes were being purchased in the election for consuls, he severely reprimanded the people and ended his speech by vowing to bring charges against those who gave the money, whoever they might be. He did, however, make an exception for

[20] **Plebeian tribuneship**: This office was open to plebeian families only, of which the Porcii Catones were one. Ten tribunes were elected annually by the plebeian assembly. Their powers varied over time, and Sulla had taken care to severely limit them, but they were restored in 75 BC, and the sacrosanctity of the office, as it had been attached to the principate by Augustus, continued throughout the Empire. The `power ... like a strong drug" to which Plutarch refers was undoubtedly its power of veto. As Plutarch explains at the end of this section, a single tribune's veto could block the actions of the consuls and other magistrates. This power and the power to introduce legislation were used to powerfully disruptive effect by Publius Clodius Pulcher, who had himself adopted by a young plebeian in order to be elected tribune for 59 BC.

Not illiberal: We have kept the characteristic double negative, of which ancient Greek and Latin and modern Romance languages still are fond when rendering praise elegantly. We have also kept the literal "illiberal" for the way it preserves the original meaning of liberal, meaning that which suits a free man, *homo liber*, as in liberal arts.

Lucania: Lucania was an ancient district in southern Italy running from Paestum on the Tyrrhenian Sea to Metapontum and Heraclea on the Gulf of Taranto. In modern Italy, it corresponds to southern Basilicata and northern Calabria.

[21] **Now, at considerable risk to himself, he entered the arena to fight for the free republic**: We are in 63 BC, the year of Cicero's consulship and the attempted coup d'état of Catiline.

Cato and Catilina Propaganda Cups
These cups, filled with food or drinks, were offered in the streets on occasion of the elections;
the cups had the name of a candidate engraved. 63 BC. The cup on the left has the inscription
asking to be elected Tribune of the plebs.

Silanus owing to their close family connection. Silanus was married to Servilia, Cato's sister. For this reason, he refrained from prosecuting Silanus, but he pursued Lucius Murena, the man whose bribes won him the consulship along with Silanus.

Now, there is **a law** that gives a defendant the right to appoint a fulltime observer over his accuser so that he might be assured that only fair and legal means are used in gathering the evidence to be brought against him. In this case, the observer assigned to Cato by Murena at first followed him very closely and observed that he was doing nothing illegal or under–handed but was instead being entirely honest and above board in gathering his evidence. Eventually, he came to admire Cato's character so much that he stopped following him and would merely stop by Cato's house on the way to the Forum and ask him if he planned to gather any evidence that day. If Cato answered no, he would simply go on his way, relying on Cato's word.

When the case finally went to trial, Cicero was consul and defended Murena. He made the judges laugh at Cato's expense with his jokes and witty mockery of **Stoic philosophers and their so–called paradoxes**. They say that Cato turned to his neighbors with a smile to say, "My, what an amusing consul we have, gentlemen!" Murena was acquitted and afterwards neither held a grudge nor acted in any way unreasonably toward Cato. On the contrary. While serving as consul, he always followed Cato's advice in matters of the highest importance and continued throughout his term in office to trust and respect him. The reason was Cato himself. Although a tough and intimidating defender of justice at court and in the Senate, outside these venues, he treated everyone with cheerful goodwill and humanity.

[22] Before becoming a tribune, Cato assisted Cicero with many of the challenges he faced as consul, but most especially in the great and noble achievement of putting an end to Catiline's conspiracy. By stirring up both sedition and open warfare, Catiline sought to bring about the total destruction of Rome. He was only **prevented from doing so by Cicero's rhetoric and by being driven out of the city.** This left Lentulus, Cethegus, and others who were also in favor of the conspiracy. They now accused Catiline of lacking boldness and courage and of being small–minded in his designs. They plotted to set the whole city

A law: Although it differs in practice, this law, both in the United States and on the continent of Europe under Napoleonic Code, still applies in principle. Both sides are obliged to share all evidence with each other.

Stoic philosophers and their so-called paradoxes: Cicero was well known for his ability to entertain the court. In the part of the *pro Murena* to which Plutarch refers (cc. 61 ff.), Cicero takes what he calls Stoic maxims or teachings (*sententiae* and *praecepta*), sets them in a real-life context, and then parodies the Stoic's reaction by exaggeration to show that it would be absurd always to act in accordance with them. They may be true when your teacher talks about them, he says to Cato, but not in real life situations (*non a natura verum sed a magistro*). For example, he introduces a Stoic saying, "that nobody is merciful but a fool and a softy," and then says, "poor folk who have suffered a calamity come begging for help." At this point he pretends to be the stern Stoic: "You would be a dastardly criminal if you ever did anything influenced by pity!" Cicero later wrote a treatise entitled The Paradoxes of the Stoics (*Paradoxa Stoicorum*) largely in praise of Cato the Younger.

[22] **Prevented from doing so by Cicero's rhetoric and driven out of the city:** Plutarch here refers to Cicero's First Catilinarian, delivered on November 8, 63 BC.

ablaze and overthrow the entire empire by means of national revolts and foreign wars. When Cicero learned of this (as I have written in his *Life*), he brought the matter before the Senate. The first to speak, Silanus, declared his opinion that these men deserved the ultimate punishment, and everyone who followed him agreed—until Caesar. Caesar was a brilliant speaker, and he regarded all **change** and disturbance of the status quo as raw material for his own designs. Rather than snuff it out, he preferred to see it grow. Rising to his feet, he spoke at length, appealing to the humanity of his listeners and saying that he would not favor killing his fellow citizens without giving them a fair trail. Instead **he moved that they be held over in prison**. So much was the opinion of the Senate overturned by this speech—and perhaps owing somewhat to its fear of the popular assembly— that even Silanus denied that he had meant the death penalty, imprisonment being **the "ultimate punishment" for a citizen of Rome**.

[23] At this moment, when all the senators began nodding agreement with the gentler and more humane position, Cato rose to speak. He began straightaway, with great conviction and anger, to abuse Silanus for changing his mind, and then pouncing on Caesar he said: "With your **popular airs** and compassionate pleading, you dare to overturn our republic and try to frighten the Senate when it is you yourself who ought to be afraid, and thankful, too, that you have escaped punishment or suspicion for what these others have plotted. How dare you so openly and boldly protect those who would destroy us while at the same time showing no pity for your own native land on the verge of destruction! Instead, you invite us to shed tears for those who should never have been born or allowed to grow up, and you mourn if by their deaths the city escapes a great massacre." This is the only speech of Cato, they say, to be preserved. The consul Cicero had instructed the most expert scribes beforehand in **a kind of shorthand,** and he had assigned them to different places around the Senate chamber. (So–called stenographers were not yet trained or used, and this, we are told, was the first use of them.) Just so, Cato carried the day. The Senate reversed course yet again and voted to put the conspirators to death.

[24] Since I don't wish to omit even those slight indications of character that complete as it were the portrait of a soul, I must include here the report that

Change: Plutarch's word is *metabole*, literally "change," but also the word he used above to signify revolution. Like Plutarch, traditional Romans called revolution "new things" (*res novae*).

He moved that they be held over in prison: According to Latin and more nearly contemporary sources (Cicero and Sallust), Caesar counseled life imprisonment in Italy and confiscation of property.

The "ultimate punishment" for a citizen of Rome: The reasoning expressed in Silanus' retraction would eventually be the pretext for Cicero's exile in 58 BC.

[23] *"Popular airs"*: *Populares* had become a political tag in the late second century BC to designate those politicians who used the tribuneship and the plebeian assembly to further legislation that favored relieving debt and limiting the power of the Senate. Those who opposed called themselves the *optimates*, meaning of the very best or the elite, but obviously without the negative connotations that that term often carries in modern democracies. The designations had little if anything to do with actual social class, as virtually all, from patrician and plebeian families alike, were very wealthy and longstanding members of the ruling class.

A kind of shorthand: Plutarch says: "in small and short signs having the force of many words." The system was invented by Cicero's slave and personal secretary, Tiro, and called Tironian notes or Tironian shorthand.

amidst all this commotion, this heated contest between Cato and Caesar, with all eyes in the Senate fixed on them, someone handed a small note to Caesar from outside. Cato immediately suspected that Caesar's allies were up to something and demanded that the note be read aloud. Caesar passed the note to Cato who was standing nearby. When Cato saw that it was a steamy love letter from his sister Servilia whom Caesar had seduced, he threw it back at him, saying, "Keep it, you drunkard!" and resumed his speech to the Senate.

On the whole, it appears that Cato was unfortunate when it came to his **womenfolk**. This sister gained a terrible reputation for the way she carried on with Caesar, while the other Servilia, Cato's **niece**, behaved even more egregiously. Having married Lucullus, a Roman of the highest renown, and having given him a son, she was later driven from his house for her licentious and promiscuous ways. But worst of all, Cato's own wife Atilia shared the same faults. Even after having produced two children with her, he was obliged to throw her out for unseemly behavior.

[25] After that, he married Marcia, the daughter of Philippus, an apparently decent woman who nonetheless occasioned much conversation due to what follows. As if in a stage drama, this part of Cato's life provides the playwright with a knotty problem difficult to untie. As told by **Thrasea, on the word of Munatius, Cato's close friend**, this is what happened. Among the many who admired and idolized Cato some were more eccentric and conspicuous in their affection than others. Among these was one **Quintus Hortensius**, a man of shining reputation and sterling character. He wished to be not only Cato's close friend and ally but also to find a way of uniting their households by establishing a kind of kinship relationship with him through marriage. To this end, **he proposed that Cato give him in marriage his daughter, Porcia**, as though she were a fertile field for his seed. One complication, however: Porcia was already married to **Bibulus** and had borne him two children. Now, this might strike most people as surpassing strange, but **Hortensius argued thus: "All of nature supports my proposal.** How can it be considered noble and natural for a woman at the peak of her childbearing years to remain idle and allow her fertility to go to waste or to allow a noble lineage to become extinct for lack of offspring? By sharing our women with worthy men, their virtues are rendered deathless and spread

[24] **Womenfolk**: Plutarch uses a word, perhaps with gentle irony, that designates the women's quarters or harem in a household.

Niece: Plutarch says "Cato's sister" but Lucullus had married Caepio's daughter, Servilia. After Caepio's death, however, she would have been in Cato's care.

[25] **Thrasea, on the word of Munatius, Cato's close friend**: P. Clodius Thrasea Paetus was a Roman senator renowned for his opposition to Nero, for which he was condemned to die in AD 66. He was committed to Stoicism, like Cato. The text of Tacitus' narrative in the *Annales* breaks off when he is about to address a Cynic philosopher Socrates–like on his deathbed. Plutarch is referring to the biography of Cato he wrote based on a book dedicated to Cato's memory by Munatius, whom we met in section [9].

Quintus Hortensius: Quintus Hortensius Hortalus, Cicero's longtime admired model and rival, would have been fifty–eight years old at the time this request was made in 56 BC.

He proposed that Cato give him in marriage his daughter, Porcia: This is a good moment to pause and be reminded of the power of the Roman paterfamilias whose authority over his children continued even after they married and had families of their own. This authority comes into play at the end of this episode when Cato calls upon Marcia's father to decide the issue.

Bibulus: Marcus Calpurnius Bibulus was Caesar's colleague and opponent in the consulship of 59 BC. He became well known that year for declaring the auspices unfavorable on a daily basis so as to provide a legal justification for voiding Caesar's decisions.

Hortensius argued thus: We have set this argument as Hortensius' direct speech, but Plutarch's Greek can be read as either reporting Hortensius' argument indirectly or expressing Plutarch's own point of view. The first option makes better reading and avoids a parenthetical argument, but the other option bears a remarkable resemblance to Plutarch's support for similar Spartan practices in his Life of Lycurgus (See *The Lawgivers*, p. 52), and it all sounds more Greek than it does Roman.

"All of nature supports my proposal": Consider how this argument might appeal to a Stoic like Cato. Another famous Stoic, the Emperor Marcus Aurelius, made a point of thanking the gods for providing him "with clear and compelling signs of what it means to live in conformity to nature." (*The Emperor's Handbook*, p. 25) For a Stoic, going against nature was not only futile but wrong.

107

throughout many families, and the bonds uniting the great families within our city are strengthened." In this way, Hortensius pressed his case, adding that if Bibulus still wanted to keep his wife, he would give her back after she gave birth. "In the end all our families—yours, Bibulus', and mine—will be brought closer together by sharing the same community of children!"

Cato answered that he loved Hortensius very much and would be delighted to see their families united, but that he considered it strange to talk about giving his married daughter to another man. As if anticipating this objection, Hortensius immediately changed tack and then made bold to ask for Cato's wife, who was still young enough to bear children and had already assured Cato's succession. Nor can it be assumed that Hortensius made this proposal thinking that Cato no longer desired his wife, for she was pregnant at this time. Cato, seeing how keen Hortensius was, could not bring himself to say no, but said instead that this idea needed the approval of Marcia's father, Philippus. So they sent for Philippus who approved of the arrangement and went so far as to pronounce the engagement in Cato's presence and with his joint sponsorship. (This all happened at a later date, but while on the subject of women, I thought it best to speak of it now.)

[26] Once Lentulus and the other conspirators had been put to death, Caesar tried to escape the accusations and charges being made against him in the Senate by taking refuge with the people and garnering support from the most noxious and destructive elements of society. Fearful of what might transpire, Cato persuaded the Senate to win over the poor and under–employed masses by distributing free grain to the annual tune of twelve hundred fifty talents. This gracious and humane action clearly averted any possible danger. Meanwhile, as soon as Metellus became a tribune, he began haranguing the assembly and proposing a law calling for Pompey the Great's return to Italy with his entire army to put down the Cataline conspiracy. This was a fine–sounding pretext, but its real purpose was to put the government in Pompey's hands and give him supreme command. When the Senate met to consider this new law, rather than attack Metellus in his usual harsh manner, Cato calmly offered much sensible advice while all the time **praising the household of the Metelli for its ancient aristocratic standing**. This only enraged Metellus who, imagining that Cato was afraid of him, began making outrageous threats and claiming that he would do as he pleased with or

[26] **Praising the household of the Metelli for its ancient aristocratic standing**: The Caecilii Metelli were one of the great aristocratic dynasties of the Roman Republic, producing at one point twelve consuls, censors, and triumphs in as many years (Syme 20). They provided core support for Sulla and as a family were decidedly *Optimates* (see note in section [23] above). Cato's point in praising the family was likely to suggest how far Q. Caecilius Metellus Nepos was going astray.

without the Senate's approval. At this point, Cato's body language, tone of voice, and language abruptly changed, and he ended his speech by saying that while he lived, Pompey would never set foot in the city with his army. The Senate now regarded both men as unhinged and not in their right minds—in an excess of evil, Metellus madly urging a policy that would bring everything to rack and ruin, and in an excess of righteousness, Cato **enthusiastically** lashing out in defense of all that is good and just.

[27] On the day when the plebeian assembly was scheduled to vote on the new law, Metellus occupied the Forum with armed foreigners, gladiators, and slaves. No small part of the people wanted the changes they hoped Pompey would bring, and they were also encouraged by Caesar, who was praetor at this time. Meanwhile, **the first citizens**, as offended by this new law as Cato, were not prepared to fight alongside him. Sensing this, Cato's entire family feared for his life. They and his friends neither ate nor slept, but spent the entire time debating what to do on his behalf. His wife and sisters in tears loudly called upon the gods while Cato, absent all fear and full of confidence, comforted and reassured them all. He took his dinner and went to bed as he was in the habit of doing and was awakened the next morning from a profound sleep by Minucius Thermus, one of his colleagues. They walked down to the Forum with a few friends and were met on the way by a great many who warned them to be on their guard. When they arrived, Cato saw the temple of the **Dioscuri** surrounded by armed men with the steps guarded by gladiators and Metellus himself seated with Caesar at the top. Turning to his friends, he said, "Look at this courageous coward who assembles an army against a single, naked, unarmed man!" and all the time walking forward with Thermus. The men guarding the steps allowed them—but only them—to pass, and with considerable difficulty and only by grabbing him by the hand was Cato able to bring **Munatius** up with him. Without hesitating, he walked right up to Metellus and Caesar and sat down between them to prevent them from talking to each other. This bold move both amazed and confounded them while some of Cato's party, seeing his confident bearing and high spirits, took heart and came closer and began shouting their support and calling upon others to stand fast and come together, not to abandon their liberty or the man who was fighting for it.

Enthusiastically: We have turned Plutarch's use of this Greek word into an adverb. It here provides a fitting example of its etymology from *en + theos*, meaning "to be possessed by a god" and in its Greek usage completely justifies the Senate's reaction.

[27] **The first citizens:** the self–styled *Optimates* or best and most distinguished men in the city.

Dioscuri: This name, a Latin transcription from the Greek meaning "Zeus' boys," designates Castor and Pollux, sons of the Spartan queen Leda with their sisters, Helen and Clytemnestra. The story of their conception involves the rape of Leda by Zeus in the form of a swan but includes mortal paternity in the form of the Spartan king Tyndareus. They were commonly regarded as half mortal and half immortal. In addition to their common role in protecting sailors, the Romans worshipped them for their help in battle. Today, the ruins of their temple in the Forum are still prominently visible beneath the Capitol where they are depicted with their horses.

Munatius: This is Munatius Rufus, not to be confused with Q. Minucius Thermus. We met Munatius, Cato's close friend and future biographer, in section [9]. He was apparently one of the "few friends" accompanying Cato mentioned above.

Dioscuri (Castor and Pollux), Capitol, Rome

Castor and Pollux Temple Forum Romanum,
Rome

[28] The clerk now picked up **the proposed law**, but Cato wouldn't allow him to read it, so Metellus took it and began reading it until Cato snatched **the tablet** away from him. Since he knew the law by heart, Metellus continued speaking until Thermus prevented him by putting his hand over his mouth. Seeing that he was losing this contest and that the people were beginning to abandon his cause, Metellus sent to his house for **soldiers**. When these arrived, rushing in shouting furiously, Cato's supporters scattered. Cato was left alone with rocks and sticks raining down upon him from above until **Murena**, someone whom Cato had once accused and taken to court, came to his rescue, shielding him with his toga and crying out to those who were throwing things to stop. Finally, putting his arm around him, he managed to convince Cato to take shelter in the temple of the Dioscuri.

Metellus, seeing the area around the speaker's platform now empty and those who opposed him fleeing through the Forum, became confident that he had won. He ordered his soldiers to retire, and he came forward calmly to conclude the passage of his law. His opponents, however, quickly recovered from their rout and advanced again, shouting boldly. So much so that Metellus' party panicked, and believing they were now under attack, fled the scene, leaving **the speaker's platform** again empty. At this point, Cato came out to encourage the people and praise their courage. The majority wanted to remove Metellus from office, and **the Senate met** to declare its support for Cato and its permanent opposition to the law that would have incited sedition and introduced civil war to Rome.

[29] But Metellus remained audacious and undeterred. Seeing that his partisans were completely panic–stricken in front of Cato and regarded him as unbeatable and impervious to violence, **he fled the Senate** and ran to the Forum where he assembled the people and launched into a bitter and insulting speech against Cato, shouting that they must flee Cato's tyranny and warning that they would soon regret dishonoring so great a man as Pompey. He then left promptly for Asia, intending to inform Pompey of how the city had wronged him.

Cato, on the other hand, received high praise and honor for having rescued the city from a treacherous tribune and for having put down in the person of Metellus the power of Pompey. His reputation was further enhanced when he pleaded successfully with the Senate not to dishonor Metellus by expelling him.

[28] **The proposed law**: From Plutarch's narrative, this would appear to be the law he describes in section [26] above, recalling Pompey with his armies to restore peace in Italy. Dio Cassius (bk. 37. c.43) adds that Cato and Thermus had vetoed the law.

The tablet: The Romans wrote letters and drafts with a stylus on light wooden tablets covered on the inside with a fine layer of wax. Two panels were joined with hinges to allow them to be closed and sealed.

Soldiers: Plutarch uses the word "hoplites" loosely here. We are dealing with private armies of thugs at this time in Rome.

Murena: The date is January 3, 62 BC Murena is now consul.

The speaker's platform: What Plutarch calls the Bema is the Rostrum in Latin, the restored remains of which are still visible in the Forum.

The Senate met: More detail about the Senate's decisions on this and the succeeding days is included in other sources, including interesting information concerning the role of Caesar, who has just assumed the praetorship. It was apparently on this day that the Senate issued a *iustitium* or state of emergency and cessation of public business, which they would mark by changing their togas. When this proved ineffective in silencing Metellus, as indicated at the beginning of the next section, they issued a "final decree," *senatus consultum ultimum*, empowering the consul to take whatever steps necessary to reestablish order. At this point, Metellus finally realized he was beaten, and rather than risk losing his life, as the famous tribune Gaius Gracchus had done, he left Rome to join Pompey in the East. While both Metellus and Caesar had been suspended from their offices, Caesar was restored and thanked by the Senate for the way he had calmed and dismissed the mob that had come to his house to support him. When he was subsequently denounced as an accomplice of Catiline, it was Cicero's evidence that had the charge dismissed and its authors punished. (See Dio Cassius 37.43ff., Suetonius's *Divus Iulius* 16–17, and CAH vol. ix, pp. 504–5)

[29] **He fled the Senate**: Literally, he suddenly (or unexpectedly) exited. This was likely to have happened after the Senate had declared the *iustitium* described in the note above, which Metellus was flaunting.

The average person admired his refusal to trample on an enemy he had completely overthrown and attributed it to his celebrated moderation and humanity. Those in the know, however, recognized his prudence and wisdom in not further aggravating the situation by **irritating Pompey**.

After that, Lucullus returned from the war in Asia. By surrendering the command and the completion of the fighting to Pompey, he was in danger of being deprived of a triumph. **Gaius Memmius** railed against him in the popular assembly and brought charges against him more as a favor to Pompey than out of any personal enmity. But Cato, being closely connected with Lucullus owing to the latter's marriage to his **sister** Servilia, angrily denounced Memmius and, for doing so, endured many insults and false accusations. Although almost being thrown out of office after being accused of tyrannical behavior, Cato eventually silenced Memmius and forced him to withdraw his accusations against Lucullus. Lucullus was then able to celebrate his triumph and henceforth grew ever more closely attached in friendship to Cato, whom he regarded as a mighty bulwark and sure defense against the power of Pompey.

[30] Pompey **the Great**, returning from the war, was convinced by the brilliance and excitement of his reception that he should be denied nothing by the people, and he sent on ahead to ask that the consular election be delayed so that he could be present to support **Piso's** bid for that office. Most of the senators were inclined to give in, except for Cato, who spoke in opposition, not so much because the delay mattered to him but because he wished to cut short Pompey's proud presumptions and designs. This caused the senators to change their minds and vote against the delay. News of this annoyed Pompey not a little, and he realized that he had little chance of achieving his aims without Cato's friendship. To this end, seeing that Cato had two marriageable nieces, he sent for his friend Munatius and commissioned him to ask for the eldest for himself and the younger for his son. (Some sources say that he courted Cato's sisters, not his nieces.) When Munatius conveyed the proposal to Cato in the presence of his wife and sisters, the women were overjoyed at the prospect of this union with so important and worthy a man, but Cato immediately took offense. Without hesitation or a second thought, he responded straight out, "Go, Munatius, go! Tell Pompey that Cato cannot be captured in the women's quarters. Cato welcomes his goodwill and

Irritating Pompey: Metellus had been relieved of his tribuneship, and exclusion from the Senate would certainly not have been unprecedented. Whether Pompey was irritated or not at Cato is a moot question. What we know for certain from Pompey's exchange of letters with Cicero is that he would try to win the support of the *Optimates* element in the Senate. Cato clearly exercised a decisive influence with that element, and it is likely that senators like Cicero attempted to steer it in Pompey's direction just as these more moderate elements tried to steer Pompey in theirs.

After that: Plutarch's phrase can hardly be turned differently. We would have to fudge the Greek to bring his narrative in line with the correct sequence of events. His narration follows events chronologically until early 62 BC during the tribuneship of Cato and suddenly we are back in 66 BC during the tribuneship of Gaius Memmius and the year of Lucullus's return from the East. Lucullus was finally awarded a triumph during Cicero's consulship in the summer of 63 BC. Plutarch's apparent understanding that Memmius and Cato were colleagues in the tribuneship and that Cato was threatened with losing his office as tribune, and not, for example, as quaestor in 65 or 64 BC, further exacerbates the problem. With section [30], we are back in 62 BC, the year of Pompey's return. In other words, even if it does not read like it, this paragraph acts as a flashback in order to give us background information of the link between Cato and Lucullus.

Gaius Memmius: Plebeian tribune in 66 BC, Gaius Memmius was the dedicatee of Lucretius's *De Rerum Natura* and himself a poet of erotic verse, according to Ovid. The poet Catullus served on his staff in Bithynia in 57—56 BC (See Catullus 28 and Quinn ad loc.).

Sister: As explained in an earlier note, this was actually Caepio's daughter, Cato's niece.

[30] **The Great**: Pompey was hailed "the Great" by his troops in Africa on Sulla's recommendation after defeating the Marian remnants at the end of the civil war. The allusion to Alexander the Great was explicit, and after his campaigns of the 60s and reorganization of the East, he appeared to have lived up to it.

"Piso's": Marcus Pupius Piso Frugi Calpurnianus had joined Sulla's camp in the First Civil War and was awarded a triumph in 69 BC for his campaign in Spain as proconsul. He was Pompey's *legatus,* second in command, in his wars against the pirates and Mithridates, and he would be elected consul in this year for 61 BC. Pompey evidently felt he needed a close associate to ratify his settlements in the East, which were considerable and would essentially remain unchanged until the end of the Republic.

assures him of a friendship more binding than a marriage alliance if he acts justly. But he will not hand over hostages to Pompey's glorification and against our country's safety."

This answer upset his womenfolk and seemed to his friends both rude and haughty. But later, Pompey supported one of his friends for the consulship by sending money to the **tribes**, flagrantly counting out the bribe in his garden. When Cato explained to the women that, had he agreed to the marriage alliance, he and his entire family would have shared in this scandal's **obloquy**, they acknowledged that he had made a wise decision by refusing. On the other hand, if we were to judge his decision based upon what later transpired, we would have to say that Cato erred in not accepting Pompey's proposals. His refusal prompted Pompey to contract a marriage with Caesar, and the combined power of those two households nearly ruined Rome and did destroy the Republic. **Perhaps none of this would have happened** had Cato, too fastidious about the small sins of Pompey, not ignored the consequences of handing power over to the greater sinner.

[31] But this was all in the future. Meanwhile, Lucullus and Pompey engaged in heated debate over **military preparations and arrangements in Pontus**, each insisting that his standing orders ought to be in force. Cato sided with Lucullus, who was clearly being wronged. Finding himself the weaker party in the Senate, Pompey played the demagogue and took his case to the people, attempting to win them over by proposing **a distribution of land for his veterans**. Cato opposed and defeated this law as well. It was at this time that Pompey formed a partnership with Clodius, the boldest of the demagogues, and drew closer to Caesar, for which Cato also paved the way. Returning from **his campaign in Iberia**, Caesar wished at one and the same time to seek a consulship and to celebrate a triumph; however, the law required those seeking the office of consul to be in the city while those preparing to celebrate a triumph to remain outside the walls. So Caesar asked the Senate to allow his friends to stand for the office in his name. Many senators were in favor, but Cato opposed the idea. Sensing Caesar's popularity in the Senate, **Cato continued speaking for the entire day and thereby defeated the motion**. Abandoning his hopes for a triumph, Caesar promptly entered the city, formed a friendship with Pompey, and campaigned for

Tribes: The Romans voted by tribe.

Obloquy: dishonor or disgrace usually resulting from strong public condemnation. The "shame storms" on social media assure us that this controversial characteristic of communal life is still alive and well.

Perhaps none of this would have happened: Given the momentous turn of events at the end of the following decade, it is virtually impossible to avoid the "what if" (or *ex post facto*, after the fact) historical judgment that Plutarch indulges in here. Indeed, the events of this section—the Senate's refusal of Pompey's request and Pompey's efforts at conciliation—have always caused later observers to wonder if Caesar's decision to cross the Rubicon and flaunt the Senate was not in some part a consequence of the lesson he learned here some dozen years earlier. After the Senate refused his request, and upon landing in Brundisium in December 62 BC, Pompey dismissed his troops and made his way to Rome to plead his own case before the Senate with reasonable hopes for success. In January 49 BC Caesar had no such hopes, remembering how the Senate had treated Pompey. Plutarch's suggestion that Cato should have seen Pompey as the lesser evil also coincides with Cicero's view at the time.

[31] **Military preparations and arrangements in Pontus**: Although it is easy to see how Lucullus was aggrieved by the three-year delay of a triumph for his military successes against Mithridates, given the Romans' readiness to grant triumphs, it is more difficult to make a case for his arrangements in Pontus. The Pontus was not definitively Roman until 63 BC, a full three years after Lucullus's departure.

A distribution of land for his veterans: Pompey's request for a grant of land to settle the thirty-five thousand to fourty thousand soldiers he had dismissed followed well-established precedents and had been facilitated by the significant increase in revenue which his Eastern settlement had created.

His campaign in Iberia: Caesar was assigned the province of Hispania Ulterior as propraetor to follow his praetorship in 62 BC. He left for Spain, where he had served as quaestor in 69 BC, and conducted military operations on the Atlantic seaboard, modern Portugal and Galicia, effectively adding these regions to the Romans' empire and reforming the debt laws. His troops hailed him as *imperator*, a highly prized honor, and he returned to Rome in June of 60 BC. As this was Caesar's first substantive military command, now nearing the age of forty, and was so successful, it is tempting to imagine that it amounted to a discovery for him.

Cato continued speaking for the entire day and thereby defeated the motion: The ancient art of filibuster.

the consulship. Once elected consul, he married his daughter Julia to Pompey. Now standing together against the State, the one proposed **laws granting the poor a colony and a distribution of land** while the other was present to support this proposal. Lucullus and Cicero, along with their followers, joined the other consul Bibulus in opposing this proposal; but foremost in opposition was Cato, who distrusted the alliance and friendship between Caesar and Pompey and regarded it with deep suspicion. He used to say that he wasn't opposed to helping the common folk through a distribution of lands, but he feared the price these men would extract as their reward by pandering and ingratiating themselves to the people.

[32] Cato's speech won over a majority in the Senate as well as many outside the Senate who found Caesar's outlandish tactics unbearable. In his brazen attempts to flatter the multitude, he adopted the methods of the most disreputable and arrogant tribunes and shamelessly used his consular authority to seduce the common people. Afraid that their proposal would not succeed on its merits, Caesar's party resorted to violence. First, they dropped a basket of excrement on Bibulus as he walked down to the Forum. Then, they attacked his **lictors** and smashed their **fasces**. And finally, they threw spears, wounding many, and drove from the Forum those who opposed the new laws. Cato, the last to leave, walked out slowly and turned around to scold and condemn the citizens for their behavior. Those who remained not only ratified the distribution of land, but decreed that the entire Senate swear to uphold the new law and defend it against anyone who might attempt to change it. The decree also inflicted serious penalties on those who refused to swear. So, all the senators swore out of necessity, remembering the fate of **the elder Metellus**, who, in former times, was forced to leave Italy for refusing to swear under compulsion to a similar law.

The women in Cato's house begged him in tears to swear the oath, and his friends entreated him to do the same. But the person who finally persuaded him to take the oath was the orator Cicero. He argued that once a decision is taken in common it is not right for an individual to go against it. Moreover, it was utterly pointless and mad to throw away his safety when it was impossible to change what had already been done.

"It would be the worst of evils if you now abandoned the State for which you

Laws granting the poor a colony and a division of land: The *Lex Iulia agraria* was voted in March of 59 BC.

[32] **Lictors . . . fasces**: Lictors were bodyguards assigned to magistrates who held *imperium* (the right to issue orders, to command) and so to consuls and praetors and to proconsuls and propraetors in command of legions. They carried **fasces**, a bound bundle of sticks topped by an axe head, the visible symbol of *imperium*. In modern times, radical groups in Italy used the word *fascio* (Italian for fasces) to describe themselves as tightly bound action groups in the late nineteenth century and used the fasces as their symbol. By 1915, Mussolini, the leader of the Fasci d'Azione Rivolutionaria, and his followers were using the word fascism to describe their ideology and fascists to describe themselves, which eventually gave us the modern origins of these words in English to designate similar ideologies and their adherents.

The elder Metellus: Q. Caecilius Metellus Numidicus, consul in 109 BC, was exiled in 100 BC for refusing to support the agrarian law of Saturninus in support of Marius, Caesar's uncle.

Universal PD

Standing Man Carrying Fasces and Arms,
Francois Boucher (1703–1770). The Met.
Universal PD

have done so much and were to hand it over to those who plot against her. Cato may not need Rome, but Rome needs Cato! All your friends need you; I most of all." (In fact, **Cicero was at this time being attacked by the tribune** Clodius, who openly plotted against him.)

By these and similar arguments, they say, and softened by entreaties at home and in the Forum, Cato reluctantly took the oath. Except for one of his close friends, Favonius, he was the last senator to do so.

[33] Caesar, flushed with his success, now proposed **another law to distribute nearly the whole of Campania to the poor and needy**. Nobody except Cato dared to speak against this law. Caesar hauled him from the speaker's platform to prison, but not even this silenced Cato, who remained as outspoken as ever, advising the people to oppose the law and urging Caesar to change his political course. The Senate and the best citizens watched all this with downcast eyes and silent grief. Their dismay did not escape Caesar's notice, but he was fixated on winning and expected that Cato would either petition him or the assembly for release from prison. When it became obvious that Cato had no intention of doing either, ashamed of what he had done and of what the people thought of it, he secretly asked one of the tribunes to obtain Cato's release.

By means of these laws, the mob was tamed, and **they voted to give Caesar the province of Illyria and all of Gaul** with four legions for five years—Cato all the while warning that they were handing over their citadel to a tyrant. Meanwhile, they elected Publius Clodius tribune, who had **illegally** changed from patrician to plebeian because he promised to do whatever they asked so long as they allowed him to banish Cicero. For consuls, they elected Calpurnius Piso, the father of Caesar's wife, and **Aulus Gabinius,** a member of Pompey's inner circle who, as they say, had intimate knowledge of his character and lifestyle.

[34] Although **they** were now firmly in control, thanks to the gratitude of the common people and the fear of the best citizens, they were still afraid of Cato. They felt discomfort and not a little shame whenever in his presence. The memory of having to use violence to overcome him was particularly annoying and irksome. And even Clodius despaired of getting rid of Cicero as long as Cato was around. Accordingly, he hatched up this scheme. As soon as he assumed the

Cicero was at this time being attacked by the tribune Clodius: Clodius assumed the tribuneship on November 16th 59 BC. As noted by Plutarch below, Clodius would eventually succeed in securing Cicero's exile in 58 BC (See also note at the end of section [22]).

[33] **Another law to distribute nearly the whole of Campania to the poor and needy**: This supplementary legislation, known as the Lex Campana, was apparently needed because the Lex Iulia had not provided enough land to house all of Pompey's veterans, who were given priority to the Campanian lots along with fathers of three or more children. As noted by Plutarch here, despite the resistance of Cato, this law passed far more easily than the *Lex Iulia* and its implementation was overseen by Pompey. Campania, the region around Naples, was highly prized for its fertility and climate by the Roman aristocracy. It should be noted, however, that Plutarch's "nearly the whole of Campania" is a gross exaggeration. Both laws designated only public lands, which the treasury at this time could easily afford. They were in fact more modest in scope than the agrarian legislation of 63 BC, and they finally solved the problem of settling Pompey's veterans (See CAH iv. 515 ff).

They voted to give Caesar the province of Illyria and all of Gaul: In hindsight, this act was, of course, momentous. Plutarch does not name his subject, but here and in the votes that close the paragraph, he seems to be designating the supporters of Caesar, or of Caesar and Pompey. It was the tribune Vatinius who proposed the legislation, the *Lex Vatinia de Caesaris Provincia*, to the popular assembly in May or June of 59 BC, bypassing the Senate. It was, however, the Senate that soon afterwards, upon the death of Metellus Celer, added his vacant province, Transalpine Gaul, to Caesar's commission, making it Plutarch's "the whole of Gaul." It was, of course, to extend Transalpine Gaul that Caesar's Gallic Wars would be fought.

Illegally: It should be noted, however, that, in section [40] below, Cato will contradict this claim in his public argument with Cicero.

Aulus Gabinius: Aulus Gabinius was the author of the *Lex Gabinia* in 67 BC that conferred on Pompey the extraordinary command against piracy that would eventually lead to his conquests and reorganization of the entire Eastern Mediterranean.

[34] **They**: Again, Plutarch declines to specify by name, but when he does so in the next section, it will be Pompey and Caesar. Some will be tempted to say "the triumvirs," or Pompey, Caesar, and Crassus, but that is a later designation made by comparison to the official triumvirate of Marc Antony, Octavian, and Lepidus. In the so–called first triumvirate, Crassus, like Lepidus later, was clearly the odd man out in terms of their internal power struggle, but his wealth was already proverbial, and Caesar was, at this point, hugely indebted to him.

office of tribune, he sent for Cato and told him, "Of all the Romans, I consider you to be the most incorruptible, and I'm prepared to act upon my trust in you. I'm besieged on all sides by men asking to be sent on the mission to **Cyprus and Ptolemy**, but you alone are the man deserving of it, and I intend to give you the favor of this appointment."

Cato responded angrily, saying that this offer was an insulting ambush, not a favor! Then in a haughty and disdainful voice, Clodius replied, "Fine! If you don't wish to accept this as a favor, you can sail to Cyprus whining all the way." And proceeding straight to the assembly, he had a law ratified sending Cato to Cyprus. For his trip, he gave him neither a boat nor a soldier nor any servants except two secretaries, one of whom was a thief and thoroughgoing rascal and the other a client of Clodius. Inasmuch as this was a small mission, and wishing to keep Cato occupied and out of the way for as long as possible during his year in office, he also ordered him to transport **refugees from Byzantium**.

[35] Before being "exiled" and knowing that Cicero was Clodius' next target, Cato advised his friend not to risk a civil war by offering resistance but to acquiesce for the moment so as later to become once again **the country's savior**. He sent his friend Canidius on ahead to Cyprus to persuade Ptolemy to stand down without a battle, promising him in return no lack of wealth or honor by giving him the priesthood of **the goddess at Paphos**. While awaiting his response, Cato stayed in Rhodes making preparations.

Meanwhile, Ptolemy Auletes, the king of Egypt, owing to **some angry disagreement** with his subjects, had left Alexandria for Rome where he hoped Pompey and Caesar would restore him to his throne by sending a Roman army back with him. On his way, he sent word to Cato, whom he asked to come and see him. As it happened, Cato was in the midst of a cleansing treatment for his colon and invited Ptolemy to come to him if he wished. When he arrived, Cato did not go out to meet him or stand when he entered the room but rather greeted him as an equal and invited him to take a seat. This at first flustered Ptolemy, who was thrown off balance by the unexpected combination of Cato's gruff and haughty manner and his simple and unpretentious greeting. But when he began discussing his situation with Cato, he heard only words full of good sense and candor. Cato rebuked him for the course he was on and admonished him not

Cyprus and Ptolemy: The younger brother of Ptolemy, Auletes of Egypt, was the king of Cyprus. A law had been passed with the intention of putting Cyprus under direct Roman control.

Refugees from Byzantium: As we discover in section [36] below, there had been some sort of civil unrest in Byzantium, and these must have been pro–Roman elements who were banished or fleeing the city owing to a change of regime.

[35] **The country's savior:** Cicero had been granted the title *pater patriae* (father of the fatherland) for his role in putting down the Catilinarian Conspiracy.

The goddess at Paphos: Aphrodite was born:—arose from the foam:—in the sea off the coast of Paphos in Cyprus.

Some angry disagreement: His subjects had revolted, and his daughter Berenice IV was on the throne.

to abandon his present happiness in order to submit himself to all the demeaning procedures, humiliations, bribe–taking, and avarice of Rome's most powerful men, whose greed all of Egypt turned to gold could not satisfy. He advised him to sail back home and be reconciled with his subjects, offering even to sail with him and help remediate his situation. These words brought Ptolemy to his senses, as if out of a fit of madness or delirium, and, recognizing the wisdom in Cato's words, he resolved to follow his advice. But his friends convinced him otherwise, and he proceeded to Rome where, as he waited to speak to a magistrate, he began to regret his decision to scorn, as it seemed to him, not so much the words of a good and wise man as the oracle of a god.

[36] By a stroke of good luck for Cato, the other Ptolemy in Cyprus poisoned himself. This came at a time when Cato was planning to sail to Byzantium. Since it was reported that Ptolemy had left a large fortune and Cato did not entirely trust Canidius, he sent **his nephew Brutus** to Cyprus. After reconciling the refugees and restoring harmony in Byzantium, Cato sailed back to Cyprus where he found a great deal of royal treasure—drinking cups, tables, precious stones, purple cloth—that had to be sold and turned into coin. Wishing to make a precise accounting and to sell everything at the highest price, he took a personal interest in every detail and drew up an exact inventory. He did not trust the usual methods of the marketplace and suspected everyone: workers, criers, sellers, and even his friends. In the end, he negotiated with the buyers directly, demanding from each of them the highest bid, and in this way he sold off most of the marketable property. His lack of trust shocked all his friends, and most especially his closest friend, Munatius. It threw him into an almost incurable rage and **provided Caesar** with the harshest criticism he makes in his tract against Cato.

[37] But Munatius wrote that the cause of his quarrel with Cato was not the latter's mistrust, but his failure to place a high value on their friendship and, in part, his own jealousy of Canidius. In his memoir concerning Cato, Thrasea's primary source, Munatius, says that when he arrived in Cyprus, he received a lodging that no one else wanted. He then knocked on Cato's door but was turned away, being told that Cato was occupied in a private conversation with Canidius. When he afterwards mildly complained of this to Cato, he received this harsh response, "'Loving too

[36] **His nephew Brutus**: This is the famous Marcus Junius Brutus of whom we will hear later. He was the son of Cato's half-sister, Servilia.

Provided Caesar: See Plutarch's explanation in section [37] below and the note on Munatius and his biographical memoir in section [25] above.

much,' as **Theophrastus** says, 'can become a source of hatred.' So it is with you who by loving me so much think that I honor you too little, and you grow angry. I employ Canidius because he is both hardworking and trustworthy. He has been with me from the start and has proven faultless." Cato later reported this private exchange to Canidius. When he learned of this, Munatius would no longer accept invitations to dine or to meet with Cato. When Cato threatened to fine him, as was the custom for those who disobeyed, Munatius paid no attention and returned to Rome and nursed his fury for a long time.

When both were back in Rome, Marcia (**who still lived with Cato**) arranged for one Barca to invite them both to dinner. Upon arriving late and seeing the others already reclining at table, Cato asked his host where he should recline. "Wherever you like," Barca replied. Looking around, Cato said, "Next to Munatius," and circling around the room he reclined next to him, but otherwise paid no special attention to him for the rest of the meal. Yet another time, again at Marcia's urging, Cato wrote to Munatius saying that he'd like to see him. Munatius came to the house at dawn, and Marcia wouldn't let him leave until all the others had left. Cato then walked in and, throwing both arms around him, greeted him affectionately. I have recounted these things in detail because I am of the opinion that in them more than in grand gestures and great public actions the true character and essential qualities of a man are revealed.

[38] Cato collected a little less than seven thousand talents of silver from the sale of Ptolemy's property. Concerned about the vicissitudes of such a long voyage, he prepared a number of jars each containing two hundred and fifty talents and each jar attached to a long cord at the end of which was fixed a sufficiently large cork so that, if the ship broke up, the buoy would indicate where the jars lay on the sea floor. As a result, almost all the silver arrived safely; however, neither of the two scrolls on which he had made copies of his exact accounts made it. His freedman Philargyrus set out from Kenchreai, the eastern port of Corinth, with one of the scrolls, and his ship capsized, and all its cargo was lost. Cato guarded the other scroll himself, and it was with him when he pitched his tent in the Forum in Corcyra (Corfu). Because of the cold there, the sailors lit several fires during the night, and the scroll disappeared when the tents caught on fire. Although Ptolemy's royal administrators were on hand to bear witness to his honesty,

[37] `**Theophrastus**`: Theophrastus was a student of Aristotle and became Head of the Lyceum in 323 BC. His *Characters* are extant and provide insightful detail into Greek notions of virtues and vices as well as probably reflecting some of Aristotle's less formal teaching. For students of Greek, by the by, they provide wonderful early texts to read in the original.

Who still lived with Cato: Before marrying Hortensius, that is (see section [25]). Cato is back in Rome in 56 BC, the same year in which Hortensius is supposed to have made his proposal.

thereby silencing his enemies and the rumormongers, the loss really upset him. It seemed as if the great pride he took in having made such careful accounts—not so much to give evidence of his credibility as to provide a model of accuracy for others—was now being **punished** by the gods.

[39] News of his arrival did not go unnoticed in Rome. All the magistrates, the priests, the entire Senate, and a large part of the populace streamed down to the river to meet him. Crowds covered both banks of the Tiber, and the proud spectacle of his boat gliding up the river was nothing short of a triumph. To some, however, it appeared ill–mannered and prideful, with **consuls and praetors** present, when he failed to disembark to meet them or at least pause to salute them but instead moved quickly past in **a royal vessel with six banks of oars**, not stopping until his entire fleet reached the docks. Nevertheless, when the treasure was transported through the Forum, the people marveled at its size, and the Senate met and voted him the usual honors, including an extraordinary praetorship and permission to attend public spectacles adorned in a purple–bordered toga. Cato declined all these honors, but he asked the Senate to grant Nicias, the manager of Ptolemy's estate, his freedom by testifying to his careful management and trustworthiness. Philippus, Marcia's father, was consul that year, and in some respects Cato shared in the power and authority of that office inasmuch as the other consul that year honored Cato as much for his virtue as for his family connection with Philippus.

[40] After Cicero returned from the exile imposed on him by Clodius, he became very powerful. Now, in the absence of Clodius, he had the **tribunician tablets inscribed on the Capitol** during Clodius' tribuneship torn down and destroyed. Clodius naturally objected, and the Senate met to discuss the matter. Cicero argued that, since Clodius had become tribune illegally, whatever he did or wrote during his time in office should be null and void. Cato kept interrupting him and finally rose to speak, saying that while he in no way approved of what Clodius did as tribune, taking away everything he did would mean taking away everything Cato had accomplished in Cyprus. His mission would be unlawful if the person who sent him did not have the lawful authority to do so. Also, he argued that the patrician Clodius had the right to be tribune since **the law granted him the right** to be adopted by a plebeian family. If he had acted improperly as tribune, he

[38] **Punished:** Plutarch uses a verb with **nemesis** at its root, a word that originally expressed the notion of divine anger or punishment. We still use the word to describe someone or something that causes one's downfall or cannot be beaten.

[39] **Consuls and praetors**: Plutarch uses the term "generals" to designate the Roman offices that correspond to that role when on campaign.

A royal vessel with six banks of oars: This appears to have been either a trireme with two rowers per oar or more likely a trireme used as a flagship fixed with towers and extra rows of oarsmen. Cato's "fleet" would have sailed into Rome's sea–faring port, Ostia, where they would have disembarked and then taken smaller rowed vessels up the Tiber to Rome, a trip that took hauled barges two to three days. Given the description of his grand arrival, Cato's boats would have come all the way up the Tiber, past the larger commercial Emporium below the Aventine to the Portus Tiburinus next to the Forum Boarium and a short walk from the main Forum.

[40] **Tribunician tablets inscribed on the Capitol:** Laws and edicts were inscribed on tablets and placed on the Capitolium.

The law granted him the right: As noted above in section [33], Cato here contradicts what Plutarch says about Clodius' change of status there.

ought to be punished for what he did, as others have been, but the authority of the office should not be called into question for the crimes of the officer. This made Cicero angry, and for a long time, he bore a grudge against Cato, but eventually they were reconciled.

[41] **In the meantime, Pompey and Crassus met with Caesar**, who had crossed the Alps. They made a pact to seek a second consulship together and, once in office, to extend Caesar's command in Gaul while assuming for themselves the most important proconsulships (Spain and Syria) along with the monies and armies to support them. This amounted to a conspiracy to divide up the empire among themselves and to destroy the Republic. Many good men were planning to stand for the consulship that year, but when they saw these two formidable competitors in the running, they changed their minds, all except for **Lucius Domitius Ahenobarbus,** who was married to Cato's sister, Porcia. Cato convinced him not to stand down or give way, saying that this was not a fight for an office but for the liberty of Rome. There was also, at this time, a general belief among Rome's most sober citizens that the concentration of power resulting from the combination of both Crassus and Pompey would prove unbearable and endanger the state. One of them should be denied. These citizens stood by Domitius and encouraged him to stay in the race, assuring him that he would receive many votes from those who were now silent out of fear.

Fearing precisely this, Pompey's men laid a trap for Domitius as he was walking at dawn with torches to the **Campus Martius**. The first man walking ahead of Domitius to light the way was struck and fell dead. After him, others were wounded and began to run away. Only Cato and Domitius stood their ground. Even though wounded in the arm, Cato held on to Domitius and urged him not to flee while calling to the others to come back and defend their liberty against these tyrants, who were now plainly showing how they intended to use their powers once in office.

[42] Domitius, unwilling to face the danger any longer, finally gave up and took refuge in his house, and **Pompey and Crassus were elected consuls**. But Cato did not give up. He decided to seek the **praetorship,** wishing to have a secure platform from which to oppose the new consuls and reasoning that he would have

[41] **In the meantime, Pompey and Crassus met with Caesar**: This was the conference of Luca in mid April 56 BC. Earlier that year, there had been bad blood between Crassus and Pompey, exacerbated by Clodius, thought to be Caesar's and Crassus' henchman. After an outburst by Pompey against Crassus in the Senate, Cicero attempted to exploit the rift while Domitius Ahenobarbus announced his intention of standing for the consulship of 55 BC and depriving Caesar of his command. Crassus went to meet Caesar, who had crossed into Cisalpine Gaul. Meanwhile, Pompey, who had been given another extraordinary command to deal with a grain supply crisis, was stopping in Pisa on his way to Sardinia. Caesar and Crassus crossed the Apennines to Luca, a town close to Pisa but still in Caesar's province of Cisalpine Gaul. This conference essentially set the stage for the Civil War to follow. Caesar would be enabled to complete his conquest of Gaul, Pompey held the two Spains with proconsular *imperium* and exercised a controlling influence on Roman politics, while Crassus obtained Syria, from which to launch his campaign against the Parthian Empire of ancient Iran. Crassus would die fighting the Parthians in 53, and Caesar would cross the Rubicon with his legions in 49 BC, launching his civil war with Pompey.

Lucius Domitius Ahenobarbus: See the note above. L. Domitius Ahenobarbus would be elected consul for the year 54 BC.

Campus Martius: Owing its name to its original use as the recruiting and training grounds for Roman troops, it was a publicly owned area still outside the legal city limit (*pomerium*) of approximately six hundred acres lying north of the Capitol. Today, it corresponds roughly to what is known as Centro, Rome's commercial center.

[42] **Pompey and Crassus were elected consuls**: Pompey and Crassus were not elected until an *interregnum* in January of 55 BC. The consul Cn. Lentulus Marcellinus refused to allow their names on the pretext that they had been handed in too late. As a counter-measure, Pompey and Crassus had a tribune veto the elections for the remainder of Marcellinus' consulship, thereby allowing their names to be entered during the interregnum that followed.

Praetorship: As we learned in section [39], the Senate had offered Cato an extraordinary praetorship upon his return from Cyprus in 56 BC, which Cato turned down. As the second highest-ranking magistrate and penultimate step in the *cursus honorum*, praetors were granted *imperium*, the power to issue orders, and were accompanied by lictors as a protection and sign of their authority. The role of the praetor in Rome was largely to preside over trials, and the office made holders eligible for Senatorial appointments to provincial commands as propraetors in the year or two following.

The maneuvers that Plutarch proceeds to recount might require a bit of explanation. We are now early in the year 55 BC and Cato is hoping to gain a praetorship for that year. Cato's chances would have been greatly increased by having one of the designated praetors disqualified during a period of sixty days in conformity with an amendment to a *Senatus Consultum* that had been passed on February 11 (See Cicero's letter to his brother Quintus 2.7.3). But as Cicero notes in his letter to his brother, the consuls, Pompey and Crassus, whose job it was, neglected to apply the Senate's decree, thereby cutting off Cato's chances for that year. But if Plutarch's account is to be trusted, Cato still stood a chance to be elected and was only ultimately thwarted by Pompey's intervention on a religious pretext. Cato would eventually be elected praetor for 54 BC.

a greater voice as a magistrate than as a private citizen. Suspecting that this was his motive and that Cato in the office of praetor would interfere with their plans, the new consuls hurriedly—and without giving notice to a great many senators— assembled the Senate and pushed through a decree that all elected praetors must assume office immediately and without the waiting period required by law in which those accused of having attained their office through bribery could be tried in court. Now, having by this decree given license to bribery, the consuls supported their underlings and friends for the praetorship, paying out handsomely and taking charge of the voting themselves. But Cato's virtuous renown overcame even these corrupt stratagems.

Most citizens regarded it as shameful and a very dangerous precedent for money to be spent to defeat Cato. It would be better to spend money electing him! Indeed, the **first tribe to cast its vote** did elect him. It was at this point that Pompey intervened, breaking up the assembly by shamelessly lying and declaring that he had heard thunder. The deeply superstitious Romans regarded this as a bad omen. No business can be concluded when a sign from Jupiter occurs until after expiation is sought and secured. By the time these ceremonies were concluded, the consuls' men were able to distribute even larger bribes and chase the best citizens from the Campus Martius. In this way, by means of violence, they got their man **Vatinius** elected praetor in place of Cato. When this announcement was made, it is said, those who had cast illegal or dishonest votes fled the scene like runaway slaves while those who remained angrily demanded that the tribune call an assembly on the spot. Cato then spoke, as if inspired by the gods, predicting the calamities that would befall the State and warning against Pompey and Crassus who, knowing that Cato was aware of their nefarious plans, feared him as praetor. After speaking, he left to go home and was accompanied by a larger crowd of citizens than escorted all the new praetors taken together.

[43] Gaius Trebonius proposed a law assigning provinces to the consuls, assigning to the one Spain and Libya and to the other Syria and Egypt, along with the naval and land forces necessary to wage war and conquer whomever they wished. Everyone despaired of being able to put a stop to this, and no one dared say a word against it. But Cato, before the voting began, indicated his desire to speak by mounting the speaker's platform, and with some difficulty, he was finally granted

First tribe to cast its vote: The assembly voted by tribe, a majority vote within the tribe determining the tribe's vote. There were thirty–five tribes based on place of residence, and the order of voting was determined by lot.

Vatinius: As tribune in 59 BC Vatinius had by the *Lex Vatinia* procured for Caesar the provinces of Cisalpine Gaul and Illyricum.

no more than two hours to speak. He used up his time touching on several subjects while trying to reason with them and making predictions about the future course of events. Although they tried to stop him from continuing, he refused to vacate the platform. A lictor then dragged him down from the platform, but he continued to speak in a loud voice from below, surrounded by a boisterous audience that joined in his grievances. The lictor then grabbed him again and dragged him out of the Forum, but as soon as he broke loose, he rushed back in and tried to mount the speaker's platform again while loudly calling upon the citizens to defend him and allow him to speak. This went on for some time until Trebonius, furious, ordered him to be led to prison. A large crowd followed him out and continued to listen to him as he made his way until Trebonius, afraid of where all this might lead, ordered him to be released. In this way, Cato used up the entire day and put off the vote.

On the days that followed, however, the consuls' men succeeded in intimidating some of the citizens while winning over others with favors and handouts. They used armed guards to prevent **Aquilius**, one of the tribunes, from leaving the Senate, and they threw Cato, while shouting that he heard thunder, out of the Forum. Many were wounded and some even killed. And so, with the liberal use of violence, they passed the law. This so incensed the people that they got together to topple Pompey's statues, but Cato, getting wind of this, prevented them from doing so.

When another law was proposed concerning Caesar's provinces and armies, Cato turned not to the assembly but to Pompey, calling upon the gods to bear witness: "You are confident now to hoist Caesar upon your shoulders and cannot foresee the day when he will become too heavy for you, and when that day comes, you will not be able to carry him or to put him down. And he will crush you and the State along with you. And then you will remember Cato's words and recognize that they were spoken no less in the interest of Pompey than in the interest of truth and justice." Pompey often heard warnings like this, but he paid no attention to them, convinced of Caesar's constancy and confident in his own power and good fortune.

[43] **Aquilius:** Publius Aquillius Gallus. From Dio Cassius (39.36), we learn that Gallus spent the night in the Senate house in order not to be prevented from entering the Forum the next day by those who had occupied it that night. Some of Cato's allies managed to sneak into the Forum the next day, among them Favonius, whom we met in section [32] and will meet in more detail in [46]. Favonius was also granted an hour to speak on the previous day. In Dio's account, Cato and Ateius were blocked from entering the Forum but managed to make themselves heard reporting thunder by being hoisted on people's shoulders outside. There was widespread corruption, riots, hired thugs. We are getting a very good picture of politics in the late Republic.

[44] The following year, Cato was made praetor. Rather than add to the dignity of the office by presiding nobly, he seems to have disgraced it by his strange behavior. He would often arrive at court barefoot and without his tunic, and dressed in this careless manner, he would pass judgment on well–known men charged with capital crimes. Some have said that he even conducted business after drinking wine at breakfast, but this is not true.

Offices at this time were commonly attained through bribery, and there were always votes for sale. Cato was determined to cure the State of this disease, and to that end he persuaded the Senate to pass a law requiring even newly elected magistrates who were not charged with distributing bribes to appear before a sworn court and open their accounts. This new law annoyed office seekers and infuriated the crowd hoping to sell their votes. So much so that, one morning, while Cato was on his way to court, an angry mob assaulted him, shouting insults and throwing stones. Everyone fled the court, and Cato, shoving and pushing his way through the crowd, barely managed to reach **his tribunal**. Standing on the dais, gazing out at the crowd with a severe and fearless look, he quickly mastered the disturbance and put an end to the shouting. By speaking firmly and reasonably, his words commanded the crowd's attention and calmed the storm. When the Senate later congratulated him for settling the crowd, he responded by saying, "Well, I cannot congratulate you for abandoning a praetor and failing to come to his defense."

Meanwhile, everyone seeking public office felt caught in a quandary, afraid of engaging in bribery yet fearful of others doing so and being deprived of office. They therefore met and decided to each deposit **one hundred twenty-five thousand drachmas** and then to seek office honestly and justly. Anyone caught paying a bribe would forfeit his deposit. Having agreed, they chose Cato to hold their deposits and arbitrate the agreement. They brought their money to him and drew up contracts in his presence, but he refused to take their money and took their promissory notes instead. When the day came to ratify the vote, Cato stood beside the presiding tribune and observed the voting. He discovered one of the candidates cheating and ordered him to pay the others. The others praised Cato for his justice but considered the conviction for cheating penalty enough and decided to cancel the fine.

[44] **His tribunal**: For the configuration of the courts in Rome, see the note on the Basilica Porcia in section [5] above.

One hundred twenty-five thousand drachmas: This sum, the equivalent of five hundred thousand Roman sesterces, as well as Plutarch's account in general, is confirmed by one of Cicero's letters to his close friend Atticus (4.15). Atticus was a wealthy Roman banker and patron of the arts. Their correspondence forms one of the best first-hand accounts we have for this period in Roman history.

Cato didn't win praise from everyone, however. Many envied him and felt he had **usurped the power of the Senate, the judges, and the magistrates. There is, after all, no virtue that invites more jealousy from others than justice** because most people find it particularly attractive. They not only honor the just man, as they do the brave, or admire him, as they do the clever, but they also love him, rely on him, and trust him. The brave they also fear. The clever they also mistrust. And they consider that the superiority of these qualities stems more from nature than free choice, chalking bravery up to a natural high spiritedness and cleverness up to **mental** capacity. Justice, on the other hand, is a virtue within everyone's reach. You can be fair whenever you choose to be. This makes injustice the most inexcusable vice and justice the most enviable virtue.

[45] This is why every powerful man hated Cato: **His virtue put them to the test**. Pompey in particular looked upon Cato's unblemished reputation as a check to his power, and he constantly sent out his people to dog and abuse him. The demagogue Clodius, once again sidling up to Pompey, was one of these. He now openly accused Cato of having made off with a lot of money from Cyprus and of waging war against Pompey because he had refused to marry Cato's daughter. Cato responded by saying that, having left for Cyprus without a single horse or soldier, he brought back from Cyprus a great deal of treasure for the State, **more than Pompey** with all his State–financed armies had brought back after ransacking the entire world. And the reason he had not chosen Pompey to be his son–in–law was not that he considered Pompey unworthy but because of the difference in their political views. "Bear in mind," he continued, "that **I declined the provincial command** I was offered after my praetorship. Pompey, on the other hand, has grabbed and held onto many provinces for himself as well as parceling them out to his friends. And most recently, he has given Caesar an army of six thousand soldiers to use in Gaul, which neither Caesar asked for nor the people authorized. Soldiers, weapons, horses, as many as you like—these are now all favors exchanged between private citizens! Calling himself imperator and general, he hands off armies and provinces to others while relaxing here at home, fomenting riots and corrupting elections. Is it not obvious to all that these are his means of **courting monarchy through anarchy**?"

Usurped the power of the Senate, the judges, and the magistrates: This opinion is the one also expressed by Cicero in the letter cited above.

There is, after all, no virtue that invites more jealousy from others than justice: This aside by Plutarch is a wonderful demonstration of his attachment to the Academy and the philosophy of Plato. (In our use of "fairness" and "fair" for "justice and "just" and in our introduction of "you" in the conclusion, we have tried to bring the thought closer to home than a strictly formal translation might.)

Mental: Plutarch says "capacity of soul."

[45] **His virtue put them to the test**: Plutarch, true again to his school, uses a verb deriving from *elenchus*, the word that describes Socrates' method of cross-examination that inevitably confutes his interlocutor and renews (or not) his quest for the truth.

More than Pompey: If Cato actually said this (which we might doubt) it's a bit surprising that Plutarch doesn't comment on the gross exaggeration. Pompey's conquests and settlements in the East had actually "brought in a lump sum of twenty thousand talents to the Treasury and had increased the yearly revenue from fifty to eighty-seven million denarii." (CAH ix. p.511)

"I declined the provincial command": As will become apparent in section [48], Cato's decision was no doubt based on a good understanding of his personal strengths and on his desire to remain in Rome in the powerful role of propraetorian judge.

Courting monarchy through anarchy – If in Plutarch's mind a Roman monarchy felt more like a Greek tyranny, this observation would track well with Plato's argument in Book VIII of the Republic where democracy inevitably devolves into tyranny.

[46] This is how he defended himself against Pompey. He had a friend and admirer by the name of Marcus Favonius, who was said to be to Cato what **Apollodorus of Phaleron** was to Socrates, a passionate and excitable listener on whom the words of Socrates had the same effect as strong wine. When Favonius sought to become an aedile, he appeared to be defeated, but Cato, who was supporting him, inspected the voting tablets and noticed that all the votes were recorded in a single hand. He exposed the fraud, and the tribune annulled the election. **Favonius was later elected aedile**, and Cato assisted him with everything pertaining to that office and in particular with the theatre's shows and spectacles. In this role, he decided to award the actors with crowns of wild olive, as they do in Olympia, rather than of gold. Instead of costly gifts, he would give the Greek performers beets, lettuce, radishes, and pears, and to the Roman performers he gave jars of wine, pork, figs, cucumbers, and armloads of firewood. Some ridiculed the cheapness of these gifts, but others delighted in seeing in these gifts signs of merriment hidden under Cato's mask of dour austerity. Meanwhile, Favonius, abandoning the privilege of his office, joined the crowd and sat among the spectators, applauding Cato and shouting for him to give prizes honoring the winners and urging others to do the same. In the other theatre, Favonius' colleague Curio put on sumptuous productions, but the people left his theatre and went to the other, preferring to be entertained by the sight of Favonius playing the private citizen and Cato the producer. Cato did all this to make fun of extravagant productions, believing that a play should be something playful, performed with cheerful and modest grace and not depend for its effect on costly accoutrements and grand designs requiring the expenditure of endless effort on mere bagatelles.

[47] Some time later when Scipio, Hypsaeus, and Milo sought to become consuls, resorting not only to the, by now, customary political shenanigans—distributing gifts and paying out bribes—but openly and by means of armed slaughter audaciously provoking civil war, some people turned in desperation to Pompey and proposed that he oversee the elections. Cato at first spoke in opposition to this idea, saying, "Our laws are meant to protect Pompey, not require his protection." When the state of anarchy persisted, however, and three armed camps surrounded the Forum on a daily basis, there appeared to be no way to end it. Cato came to the conclusion that, as a last resort and temporary expedient, the

[46] **Apollodorus of Phaleron**: An exchange at the beginning of Plato's *Symposium* nicely illustrates this comparison in relation to what follows.

A's Friend:	*You're always the same, Apollodorus, always bad-mouthing yourself and others. I think you actually believe everybody except Socrates to be wretched, starting with yourself. Why sometimes you get the nickname "softy" is beyond me because in discussions you're always the same, always getting irritated at everybody except Socrates.*
Apollodorus:	*O my dear friend, is it so obvious then that when I think this way about myself and all of you that I'm raving and miss the mark?*

Favonius was later elected aedile: Favonius was elected in 53 BC to serve as aedile in 52 BC.

Senate should entrust the affairs of state to Pompey. And so, hoping by the most moderate remedy he could find to prevent the collapse of the State, he brought on monarchy because he preferred monarchy to anarchy. Thereupon **Bibulus, a relative of Cato**, brought a motion in the Senate to name Pompey as sole consul, saying that either Pompey would re–establish the rule of law, or the State would be enslaved to its most powerful citizen. Cato stood up and to everyone's surprise seconded the motion, adding that any rule was better than no rule and that he trusted Pompey to bring the present situation under control and to act in the best interest of the State.

[48] As soon as Pompey was declared consul, he invited Cato to come see him at his house outside the city limit. When he came, Pompey embraced him and, taking him by the right arm, thanked him warmly for his words in the Senate. He invited him to serve as his advisor and right–hand man in his new office. Cato responded by saying that whatever he said about Pompey on former occasions was not said out of enmity nor was what he said now meant as a personal favor but all in the best interests of the State. "In private, if asked, I will be happy to advise you; and in public, even when not asked, I will always say what I think."

And Cato did exactly as he said he would. First, when Pompey made laws creating new fines and stiff penalties for those who had paid bribes, Cato advised him not to worry about past wrongs, but to focus on the future. "Once you start looking into former crimes, you won't know where to stop; and if you apply new laws to past crimes, you will end up punishing people for misdeeds that weren't unlawful when they committed them." Later, when many well–known men were on trial, some of them friends and relatives of Pompey, and seeing Pompey weakening in his resolve to proceed with prosecution, Cato vehemently reproved and set him straight. Pompey also made a law that put an end to the custom of making speeches in praise of the accused, but he wrote such a speech on behalf of his friend **Munatius Plancus** and sent it to the court to be read at Plancus' trial. Cato happened to be one of the judges and covered his ears with his hands during the reading of it. For this, Plancus succeeded before judgment was made in having Cato recused, but the judges found him guilty anyway. In general, Cato was an insurmountable obstacle for defendants and not easily taken in by their alibis and excuses. They neither wanted him as a judge nor dared to recuse him. And not a

[47] **Bibulus, a relative of Cato**: We met Marcus Calpurnius Bibulus, Caesar's colleague and opponent in the consulship of 59 BC, in section [25] above as married to Cato's daughter, Porcia.

[48] **Munatius Plancus**: Plancus was tribune of the plebs in 52 BC and accused of helping to set fire to the Curia (Senate house), for which, see note on the Basilica Porcia in section [5].

few were condemned as a result of avoiding Cato. This made them appear not to have confidence in their innocence, and when they refused Cato as a judge, it was used against them by the prosecution.

[49] At this time, Caesar was preoccupied with his army and the fighting in Gaul and had to rely on the use of gifts and money and friends back in Rome to increase his influence in the city. These activities and Cato's old predictions began to shake Pompey's confidence in Caesar's constancy and cause him to imagine the worst. But seeing that Pompey lacked daring and was slow to move against Caesar, Cato decided to seek the consulship himself in order to deprive Caesar of his armies and expose his subversive ambitions. **His rivals** were both men of distinction. One of them, Sulpicius, owed much of his standing and influence in the city to Cato, so it seemed rather mean and ungrateful of him to stand against Cato. Cato, however, made no such complaint, saying merely, "What is so shocking about not yielding to another what you believe to be the greatest of goods?" He asked the Senate to vote that those seeking office should petition the assembly themselves and do their own canvassing **rather than employ others to solicit votes and speak on their behalf**. This was not a popular measure. Not only did it deprive the "solicitors" of a salary, it prevented the candidates from granting favors to the people. And the people were furious, seeing this as a means of both impoverishing and dishonoring them. What is more, Cato was by no means a convincing canvasser on his own behalf. He was more concerned with preserving his austere and dignified manner than with charming crowds and winning votes. So in doing his own canvassing and not allowing his friends to do the things that please and win over the crowd, he lost the consulship.

[50] Losing an election, not only for those who lose but also for their friends and family, normally brings with it a letdown and sadness, combined with a feeling of humiliation that can last for many days. But Cato seemed not to mind, and the next day, simply resumed living his life, enjoying a good rub down with oil, playing ball in the Campus Martius, and after a late breakfast, walking barefoot and tunic–less to the Forum to chat with his friends. **Cicero criticized him** for failing to pursue the consulship energetically at a time when the affairs of state demanded such a consul. He blamed him for not mingling on friendly terms with

[49] **His rivals**: Servius Sulpicius Rufus and Marcus Claudius Marcellus would be elected consuls for 51 BC . Sulpicius had acted as *interrex* in the naming of Pompey as consul in this year, and it is thought that Marcellus was likely Cato's friend and colleague in the quaestorship, who gets a mention in section [18]. Dio Cassius's account (40.58) gives us another take on the situation. For Dio, Marcellus acted in Pompey's interest and, seeking to defend the state against Caesar, sought to have Caesar replaced in Gaul whereas Sulpicius opposed Marcellus's attempt out of legal principle: It violated the law that gave Caesar his command. Cicero's letters add closer detail, including the note that Marcellus had to be brought in line by Pompey. (See ad fam. viii.2 and CAH ix p. 629)

Rather than employ others to solicit votes and speak on their behalf: On this standard Roman practice, see note on nomenclators in section [8].

[50] **Cicero criticized him**: One of the more interesting aspects of this period is the relationship between Cato and Cicero, which Plutarch touches on again here because of the light it sheds on the behavior and intentions of Pompey and Caesar.

the people and for seeming to tire of politics and giving up on the idea of running again. He even reminded him of how, after being defeated the first time, Cato had chosen to run for the praetorship a second time. To all this, Cato responded by reminding Cicero that he had not lost the praetorship the first time around in a fair election but because the people were threatened by violence and corrupted by bribes. In the recent consular election, on the other hand, no fraud had been committed, and his manner had simply rubbed people the wrong way. "What decent and sensible man will change his manner just to please others or try a second time with the same manner to suffer the same defeat?"

[51] **With extraordinary skill and against impossible odds**, Caesar was, at this time, invading and defeating many warlike peoples. Among these were **three hundred thousand Germans whom Caesar attacked and killed during a declared truce**. Caesar's friends petitioned the Senate to celebrate the good news with public sacrifices, but Cato demanded that they hand Caesar over to those he had unjustly attacked to expiate his illegal actions and prevent them from polluting the city. "Yes, let us all be thankful and sacrifice to the gods for sparing the city as well as our soldiers the gods' dread punishment for this general's insane and unconscionable behavior." Upon hearing of this, Caesar wrote a letter full of slanderous accusations against Cato and sent it to the Senate. After it was read, Cato stood up and, in a calm and easy manner, as though having anticipated and thoughtfully rehearsed what he wished to say, began to treat it all as an amusing diversion. He lightly explained that the accusations against him were just name–calling and dirty little jokes, typical of Caesar's childish and coarse humor among friends. He then went on to outline Caesar's ambitions and seditious schemes from the beginning, not as one of Caesar's enemies but rather as a friend and co–conspirator. He concluded his talk, more as a threat than as a warning, by saying, "If you are wise, it isn't the sons of the Britons or Celts whom you should fear, but the child Caesar." This speech so unnerved and stirred up the Senate that Caesar's friends regretted having read his letter to the Senate and presenting Cato with the opportunity to utter so many hard truths and just accusations. No decisions came of this, however, although it was suggested that it would be a good idea to name Caesar's successor. Caesar's friends then demanded out of fairness that Pompey should lay down his arms and give up his armies if Caesar were

[51] **With extraordinary skill and against impossible odds**: We have allowed ourselves to indulge in a lengthy rendering of Plutarch's single adverb *parabolos* in order to bring out the different uses and connotations of the word. Deriving from the verb *paraballein,* the adjective means "exposing oneself or what belongs to one" (LSJ ad loc.), hence "reckless or perilous," and the adverb is sometimes used to mean "in an extraordinary manner." In any case, here we have the conquest of Gaul in a single clause, at least up until the massacre in 55 BC of two tribes of Germans who had been driven out of their homes and had crossed the lower Rhine. By this time, Caesar had stopped a migration of some three hundred thousand Helvetii from Switzerland; defeated Germanic tribes that had established themselves in Alsace; established a key Roman defensive position in Vesontio (modern Besançon) where he definitively won over the undying loyalty of his legions; defeated a large force north of Reims that had come down from the area of modern Belgium; built a fleet on the Loire, which would eventually defeat and capture a fleet of two hundred and thirty ships of the Veneti in the first Roman naval battle in the Atlantic in Quiberon Bay, thereby securing definitive control over Armorica (modern Brittany); and was making advance preparations for his first expedition to Britain. An "extraordinary" accomplishment, indeed! But as you read what follows, keep in mind that all these actions involved staggering losses of life, hundreds of thousands of enslaved captives, and vast quantities of plunder, all hauled back to Rome in endless caravans.

Three hundred thousand Germans whom Caesar attacked and killed during a declared truce: An advance by Caesar's Gallic cavalry provoked the Germans to attack and rout them. When the German leaders came to the Roman camp to apologize, Caesar had them arrested and proceeded to attack. Even in Caesar's account, his *commentarii de Bello Gallico,* it is evident that he was seeking a pretext to break the truce, which the Germans not only obligingly provided but then tied their hands behind their backs by coming with all their leaders and their sons to Caesar's camp to apologize, obviously in hopes of extending the truce. It is tempting to think that this extract from the *commentarii* as published later in book form is essentially unchanged from Caesar's report to the Senate. We offer a translation in Appendix C. As you read, imagine you are a Senator hearing it read in the Senate chamber or perhaps a plebeian hearing it read out in the Forum by a tribune. Try to be honest with your persona: You are a Roman. How do you react, like "Caesar's friends" or like Cato? And is Cato's reaction motivated more by pity for the Germans or by his fear of Caesar?

required to do the same. At this point, Cato cried out that precisely what he had predicted had now come to pass: Caesar was now using his power in the city and the threat of his armies to oblige the Senate to do his will. But outside the Senate, Cato was powerless. The people always wanted Caesar to be the greatest, and although he convinced the Senate, the Senate feared the people.

[52] Finally, when news arrived that Ariminum [modern Rimini] had fallen and Caesar and his armies were marching toward Rome, all eyes looked to Cato, the people's as well as Pompey's, since he had warned them from the beginning and was the first to see what Caesar was really up to. "If you had believed me and heeded my advice," he told them, "you would not now be in the position of fearing only one man and putting all your hopes in another." To this, Pompey replied, "Truly, Cato has spoken like a prophet while I acted like a friend." Cato then advised the Senate to put everything in Pompey's hands, saying, "The one who has brought this crisis on the city is the only one with the power to fix it." But Pompey, finding that the forces he had were not prepared and that those he was able to recruit were not keen to fight, decided to abandon the city. Cato decided to leave with him and sent his younger son for safekeeping to Munatius in **Bruttium** and kept the oldest with him. Needing someone to manage his household and take care of his daughters, he renewed his marriage to Marcia, who was now a wealthy widow, her husband Hortensius having died and left her his fortune. Caesar later abused Cato for this, accusing him of avarice and arranging his marriages to enrich himself: "If he needed a wife, why did he give her away in the first place? And if he didn't need one, why did he take her back? Unless of course the plan all along was to use her to snare Hortensius—to make the loan of a young one and be paid back with a rich one." But **these lines from Euripides** give us a fitting response to such accusations:

> *Call Hercules a coward? That would be sacrilege!*
> *And what could be worse than sacrilege?*

After all, accusing Cato of greed amounts to the same thing as calling Hercules a coward. There may be other reasons for calling his marriage inappropriate, but that is another matter. Whatever the case, Cato remarried Marcia, entrusted his household and daughters to her, and followed Pompey into exile.

[52] **Bruttium**: Plutarch refers here to the region, the land of the Bruttians, or Bruttium as it is often called, which corresponds roughly with modern Calabria rather than to the ancient city of Bruttium.

These lines from Euripides: Plutarch quotes lines 174–175 from Euripides' *Heracles*.

[53] They say that from that day until the end of his life he never cut his hair, shaved his beard, or **wore a crown.** Whether the news was good or bad, he continued in this way as a sign of sadness and mourning for the tragic fate of his country. He was now assigned the province of Sicily and crossed the straits to Syracuse, but when he learned that **Asinius Pollio** had arrived in Messina with an army loyal to Caesar, he sent to ask why he had come. Pollio responded by asking, "Why has the government been overthrown?" When Cato learned that Pompey had quit Italy altogether and was now camped at **Dyrrachium,** he wondered aloud at the inscrutability of the gods. "Why is it that as long as Pompey acted dishonestly and unjustly, he seemed invincible, but now when he is trying to save his country and preserve her freedom, he is powerless?" He claimed that he could throw Asinius Pollio's forces out of Sicily, but knowing that a much larger army was on the way, he refused to destroy the entire island by going to war. Instead, he sailed away after advising the Syracusans to save themselves by going over to the stronger party. When he joined Pompey, he steadfastly held to the same opinion, **wishing to avoid decisive action and desiring to draw out the war in hopes of an eventual settlement**. Nor did he want to see his country ruined by the sword regardless of who turned out to be the eventual victor. He also persuaded Pompey and his advisers to adopt similar principles— not to plunder any city subject to Rome and not to kill a fellow Roman except in combat. In this way, he earned Pompey a good reputation and attracted many people to his side because of his moderation and kindliness.

[54] Later, Cato was sent to Asia to help **recruit troops and gather ships** for Pompey. He brought with him his sister Servilia along with her son by Lucullus. She was now a widow and had largely overcome the earlier **slanders concerning her licentiousness** by being in Cato's care and sharing in his travels and austere manner of life. Nevertheless, Caesar did not spare Cato and made **slanderous remarks about his sister** as well.

Cato managed to bring the people of Rhodes into Pompey's camp, and leaving his sister Servilia and her son there, he returned to Pompey, who by this time had assembled brilliant naval and land forces. It was at this moment that Pompey most clearly revealed his plans. Although Pompey's officers appeared to have no further need of Cato, Pompey himself wanted to entrust Cato with the command of his

[53] **Wore a crown**: The wearing of crowns or rings of flowers or leaves was very common in antiquity at all sorts of celebratory occasions public and private.

Asinius Pollio: Gaius Asinius Pollio is perhaps most famous as a patron of the arts, Vergil and Horace in particular. He built the first public library in Rome, the Atrium Libertatis, or Liberty Hall. This is a good example of how "liberty" is understood to be the condition that affords us the leisure to cultivate the liberal arts. It contained Greek and Latin wings and a very fine collection of Hellenistic sculpture, and he organized public readings, most famously of Vergil reading the *Aeneid*. He was himself a poet and historian and moved in the circles of Catullus in his younger years. His contemporary history is lost but was a major source for later writers, including Plutarch. He enters Plutarch's narrative here as an important supporter and commanding officer for Caesar, having joined Caesar before his decision to cross the Rubicon. Although his presence in Sicily has sometimes been doubted—he doesn't figure in Caesar's account in his *Commentarii de Bello Civili* (i.30—31)—Plutarch appears to follow Appian (and Pollio?) to say that he was sent to relieve Cato of his command. If so, it was an astute choice by Caesar, as Pollio was no hothead and known for his adherence to legality. His response here is in fact very clever, amounting to: "Yes, Cato, I am here to relieve you. The State has been overturned, but by whom?"

Dyrrachium: Modern Durres in Albania, Dyrrachium was the capital of the Epirus Nova.

Wishing to avoid decisive action and desiring to draw out the war in hopes of an eventual settlement: This strategy, if you like, bears a remarkable resemblance to General Washington's during the American Revolution. Surrounded by others who were impatient for a decisive encounter with the British forces, Washington (no doubt a reader of Plutarch's Life of Cato) believed that by keeping his ragtag army in the field and prolonging the war, the British would eventually tire and come to terms as they did at Yorktown.

[54] **Recruit troops and gather ships**: It is interesting to note that in Caesar's account (*de bello civili* i.30), the one mention of Cato's activity in Sicily compliments his industry in repairing and ordering the construction of new ships. As modern readers, we are again (see our note on denying a provincial assignment in section [45]) struck by what was clearly an appreciation on the part of Pompey and Caesar for Cato's strong suit: procurement, organization, and financial management, skills that he had demonstrated so well in his quaestorship, where he seems to have made his mark. And we will once again see below in section [58] that Metellus Scipio asks Cato to manage Utica as his supply base apparently for the same reason. Plutarch, however, will repeatedly, as in the passage immediately following, suggest that Cato was or would have been an excellent commanding officer had jealousy or his own deference not played a role. Plutarch maintains this point of view without any hard evidence that Cato was ever an effective commanding officer in battle.

Slanders concerning her licentiousness: See section [24] above.

Slanderous remarks about his sister: evidently in his *Anticatones*, on which, see our note in section [12].

entire fleet of which there were no fewer than five hundred warships along with any number of galleys, reconnaissance vessels, and open boats. But it soon occurred to him, perhaps being reminded by his friends, that Cato's sole motivation in aiding Pompey was to liberate his country. Were he to become the master of so great a force, one could be sure that on the very day they defeated Caesar he would ask Pompey to lay down his arms and put himself under the rule of law. This consideration caused him to change his mind, and although he had already broached the subject with Cato, he now named Bibulus admiral of the fleet.

In spite of this slight, Cato's zeal for the cause was in no way diminished. Before one of the battles at Dyrrachium, we are told that Pompey addressed the troops and ordered each of his generals to do the same. Passively and indifferently, the soldiers barely listened as each general spoke in turn until it became Cato's turn to speak. Unlike the rest, he spoke with the passionate intensity that came naturally to him, using the language that philosophers use concerning liberty, courage, death, and glory. In closing, he invoked the gods as if they were present and watching intently as these men struggled to free their homeland. No sooner had he finished than a mighty war cry went up, and the troops following their generals rushed headlong into battle full of death–defying hope. But even though they routed and put to flight Caesar's army, **Caesar's daemon**—taking advantage of Pompey's inveterate caution and indecision when faced with success—robbed them of the complete victory. (This is described in my *Life of Pompey*.) While the rest of the army celebrated and rejoiced in their success, Cato wept for his homeland and lamented the **daemonic ambition** that caused so many of his countrymen to murder one another.

[55] When Pompey broke camp to pursue Caesar into Thessaly, he left behind a large quantity of weaponry and money as well as many non–combatants, members of his family, and domestic servants. Because he both trusted and feared the man, he appointed Cato to take charge and guard it all with fifteen cohorts. In case he was beaten, he trusted Cato above all others to stand by him, but if victorious, Cato's presence would get in the way of using his victory as he pleased. Many other leading men were left behind with Cato in Dyrrachium. Upon learning of **the army's defeat at Pharsalus**, Cato waited for news of Pompey's fate. If Pompey was dead, he planned to take everyone in his charge to Italy and live

Caesar's daemon: It is quite clear that Plutarch shared a very real belief in a person's *daemon* as he also did in the role of Tyche or Fortune. The ancient Greeks traditionally regarded the divine power that controls an individual's destiny, for good or for ill, as his *daemon*. To Heraclitus' "A man's character is his daemon," he would probably have responded: "A man's character is the manifestation of his daemon." Caesar managed to extract his legions to their camp intact, and they gave Pompey's forces the slip the next day. Caesar's veteran legions were proverbially well trained in forced marches, and after four days, Pompey gave up his pursuit.

Daemonic ambition: A famous anecdote nicely characterizes what Cato laments. When crossing the Alps and staying in an Alpine village, Caesar is supposed to have remarked: "Better to be village chieftain here than to be second in Rome."

[55] **The army's defeat at Pharsalus**: Pompey suffered a crushing defeat at Pharsalus in Thessaly in the spring of 48 BC, with some six thousand casualties and the surrender of more than twenty-four thousand men.

in exile there as far away from Caesar's tyranny as possible. If Pompey was still alive, he would keep the army intact with him. With this plan in mind, he crossed over to Corcyra where the fleet was stationed and expected to turn his command over to Cicero, who **as consul outranked him as praetor**. But Cicero was on his way to Italy and refused the command. At this point, **Pompey's hotheaded son**, with an untimely sense of his own importance, intervened to stop anyone from sailing back to Italy, especially Cicero. But Cato spoke with him privately and calmed him down and, by doing so, clearly saved Cicero's life and prevented harm from coming to others as well.

[56] Thinking that Pompey the Great had probably taken refuge in **Africa** or Libya, Cato made haste to join him. After first releasing and leaving behind those who were not eager to continue the fight, he embarked with the rest and set sail. Cruising along the coast of Africa, he encountered Sextus, Pompey's younger son, and learned from him that **his father had died in Egypt**. Everyone bore this news very badly, and they declared that, after Pompey, they would follow no one but Cato. Out of compassion and respect for the many good men in his company, men who had proven their loyalty, and because it would have been shameful to desert them and leave them without a leader in a strange land, Cato agreed to assume command and made for the city of Cyrene where he was welcomed, even though just a few days earlier the city had shut its gates against **Labienus**. There, he learned that King Juba had received Scipio, Pompey's father-in-law, and that Attius Varus, whom Pompey had appointed governor of Africa, was with them and in possession of an army. Wanting to join up with them and since it was now winter, Cato decided to go overland, bringing with him a great many mules to carry water, a large herd of livestock, and numerous carts carrying provisions. He also brought with him some of the people called Psylloi, known for curing snakebite by sucking out venom with their mouths as well as for the spells and incantations they use to charm the snakes themselves. They marched for †**seven days**†, Cato all the time **walking** in front without riding on a horse or an ass. From the moment he learned of the defeat at Pharsalus, he ate seated rather than reclining at table, and in addition to this and other acts of mourning, he never lay down except to sleep. That winter **in Libya**, he led out an army close to 10,000 men.

As consul outranked him as praetor: Neither man was in office, of course, but these were their last and highest offices respectively.

Pompey's hotheaded son: Gnaeus Pompeius would go on to fight against Caesar in Africa and Spain and would finally be hunted down and put to death after the defeat at Munda in 45 BC.

[56] **Africa**: The region roughly corresponding to modern Tunisia and western Libya went by the name Africa.

His father had died in Egypt: Pompey was killed upon disembarking in Alexandria, evidently the work of the courtiers of Ptolemy Auletes' son, who was still a boy of nine or ten. Egypt itself was in the throes of a conflict between the young Ptolemy's supporters and his older sister Cleopatra and hers. The famous story of her encounter with Caesar will be told in Plutarch's *Life of Caesar*.

Labienus: Labienus had been Caesar's *legatus*, or second in command, in Gaul but had gone over to Pompey before the Civil War. As often seems to be the case with people who switch loyalties, he was particularly zealous in his fight against Caesar's party, feared for his execution of prisoners at Dyrrachium, and taunted for his boasting at Pharsalus. This reputation had apparently preceded him to Cyrene.

Seven days: The text appears to be corrupt at this point, and the probable correction to twenty–seven is usually accepted. The geographer Strabo says the journey took thirty days and in Lucan's account in Book 9 of his Civil War epic known as *Pharsalia*, the journey lasts two lunar cycles.

[57] **Walking**: Plutarch uses the verb from which Aristotle's school of philosophy gets the name peripatetic, from the habit of talking philosophy as they walked in the Lyceum, a public area outside the city walls in Athens.

In Libya: Cato wintered in Leptis Magna near the western frontier of Libya and proceeded to Utica in Africa in the spring of 47 BC.

[57] Things went badly with Scipio and Varus. They quarreled incessantly and competed for King Juba's favor by flattering him, making the heaviness of his arrogance unbearable and the vanity inspired by his wealth and power insupportable. When he first received Cato, he placed his seat between Scipio and Cato, taking the place of honor between the two of them. When Cato saw what was happening, he moved his chair to one side, putting Scipio in the middle even though he was a personal enemy and had written slanders against him. Those who dismiss this as an insignificant gesture are forgetting how they faulted him for once in Sicily giving up the middle place to Philostratos "out of respect for philosophy." Anyway, it was this gesture and none other that stopped Juba from treating Scipio and Varus like a couple of satraps and led to their reconciliation. The soldiers all wanted Cato to lead them, and Scipio and Varus themselves were more than happy to step aside and hand Cato the command; however, Cato refused by saying that he would not break the very laws whose lawbreaker they were fighting. (**Scipio had been named proconsul**, and it would not have been lawful for a propraetor like Cato to assume command when a proconsul was present.) In the end, the soldiers were brought around by thinking they were sure to win with **an officer named Scipio in Libya**.

[58] Scipio was no sooner named commander than, to please Juba, he announced his plan to kill all the residents of Utica of military age and to raze the city on the pretext that it had supported Caesar. Cato wouldn't hear of it! But it was only by shouting in protest and loudly invoking the gods in the war council that he managed to shield the poor citizens of Utica from the savagery of Scipio and Juba. At Scipio's request and the pleading of Utica's citizens, Cato agreed to assume the oversight of Utica so that the city would not, willingly or unwillingly, go over to Caesar. For all sorts of reasons, Utica was a very strategic place, and Cato fortified it even more. He brought in a great quantity of grain, repaired the walls, erected towers, and encircled the city with deep trenches and tall palisades. The Uticans of military age he housed inside the palisades and provided with arms. The rest of the citizens he brought inside the city's wall and took great care that they not be insulted or harmed by the Romans stationed there. To the soldiers living in the Roman encampment, he sent arms, money, and large supplies of grain, turning the entire city into one large supply base.

Scipio had been named proconsul: Metellus Scipio had been consul with Pompey in 52 BC. We met him in section [7] as the fiancé of Cato's first prospective bride, an incident that probably explains the statement that he was a "personal enemy" above.

An officer named Scipio in Libya: The Scipio name was, of course, famous in Africa owing to Publius Cornelius Scipio Africanus, who defeated Hannibal to end the Second Punic War, and his grandson by adoption, Scipio Aemilianus, who ended the Third Punic War by destroying Carthage. In his *Life of Caesar*, Plutarch also mentions the existence of an oracle stating that the Scipios would always be victorious in Africa. Metellus Scipio commanded the center for Pompey at Pharsalus and would command the Pompeian forces at Thapsus in 46 BC. After his defeat, he tried to escape to Spain. When he was overtaken by the Caesarian fleet, like Cato he would commit suicide to avoid capture.

He advised Scipio, as he had Pompey, not to engage a brilliant and battle–hardened general, but to adopt the tactics of delay and wait for the crisis to pass and the strength of the tyranny to waste away. But out of arrogance Scipio scorned this advice and wrote a letter to Cato accusing him not only of cowardice for hiding behind the city's walls but for seeking to hinder others from exercising their judgment and boldly seizing the moment. To this, Cato wrote back offering to take to Italy the infantry and cavalry he had brought with him to Libya and thereby to create a diversion and draw Caesar's army away from Scipio. But Scipio only laughed at this idea. From this moment on, Cato let it be known that he was sorry for having surrendered the command to Scipio, believing Scipio incapable of waging war intelligently, or if against all odds he were to succeed, fearing that he would fail to exercise restraint in dealing with his countrymen. He now told his friends that he viewed the outcome of the war with little hope owing to the inexperience and headlong foolhardiness of the generals. If by some stroke of luck Caesar were defeated, he said he would not remain in Rome but would flee what was certain to be the vengeful cruelty of Scipio, who had already made vicious and haughty threats against many. In the end, it turned out even worse than he had imagined it would. Just three days later, late in the evening, a messenger arrived from the camp to say that there had been **a great battle at Thapsus**. All was lost. Caesar had captured the camp. Only Scipio and Juba got away with a few others. The rest of the army was destroyed.

[59] This news, arriving at night during a time of war, naturally panicked the citizens of Utica and sent them into a frenzy. They could barely be contained within the walls of the city. Cato then went out to confront those who were running about screaming. By stopping and reasoning with them, he removed some of their more exaggerated fears, reminding them that these initial reports were probably inaccurate or incomplete. This seemed to restore a sense of calm for the moment. The next morning, he summoned to the temple of Jupiter the Three Hundred, a group of Roman businessmen and bankers living in Libya that he used as a Council along with any Senators present and their sons. As they were gathering, Cato walked among them chatting amiably as if nothing unusual had happened and reading aloud from a tablet he was carrying. It simply contained a list of supplies needed for the war: arms, grain, archers, and infantry.

[58] **A great battle at Thapsus**: As a critical reader might suspect, the Battle of Thapsus was not quite the foregone conclusion that Plutarch's account seems to describe. The Pompeian or Republican forces had in fact played Cato's waiting game for four months of cat–and–mouse maneuvers in an attempt to deprive Caesar's army of supplies and not wishing to engage his legions in a pitched battle. Caesar had just received reinforcements from Sicily and had invested the town of Thapsus, situated on the coast some two hundred miles southeast of Utica. The town faced the sea with a lagoon at its back and was reached via a western and eastern isthmus on either side. Scipio decided to attempt to trap Caesar in the town by blocking both with superior forces. The ancient accounts of the battle we have, including Plutarch's (*Caesar* [53]) if we discount the clearly false rumor that Caesar was absent owing to an epileptic fit, point to a brilliant piece of generalship on Caesar's part, ending in the overwhelming victory that Plutarch describes here.

Once everyone had gathered, he began his speech by praising the Three Hundred for their zeal and loyalty to their country, demonstrated by the generosity of their persons, money, and advice. He exhorted them to stay united and not to abandon hope by trying individually to flee the city. He assured them that by staying together Caesar would despise them less for having opposed him and would be more merciful to them as supplicants. He urged them to reason among themselves and promised that whatever course they chose, he would not hold it against them. If they changed allegiances owing to the reversal of Fortune, he would understand the wisdom of bowing to Necessity; however, if they decided to stand firm and face danger for the sake of liberty, he would not only praise them but, in admiration for their unflinching courage, would lead them into battle as well as fight side by side with them.

By choosing this latter course, he believed they would put Fortune to the test, the fortune not only of **Utica or Hadrumentum** but of Rome herself that on former occasions had stood the test of greatness and been rescued from more dire circumstances. Besides, they should consider the many circumstances that favored their salvation and safety, chief among them the fact that they were fighting against a man being threatened on many sides. Spain was already fighting on the side of the younger Pompey, and Rome itself, not yet broken and accepting of the bit and bridle, was in open revolt against any new master. "We should not run from danger but rather take a lesson from our enemy who is willing to risk everything in pursuit of the most grievous wrongs and a most uncertain outcome while we fight to preserve the blessings of liberty if we succeed and a glorious death if we fail." He finished his speech by urging them, once again, to reason among themselves and by saying that, whatever they decided, he would pray the gods to reward them for their former courage and the loyalty they had once shown to Rome.

[60] When Cato finished speaking, some found his argument persuasive and gained confidence from it, but most of his listeners were so carried away by the fearlessness and graciousness with which he spoke that they almost forgot the danger they were in. Seeing in him their only undefeated leader, a man untouched by Fortune, they begged him to employ their persons, their wealth, and their arms as he saw fit. Better to die trusting this man, they thought, than to save

[59] **Utica or Hadrumentum**: Hadrumentum was the capital of Byzacium and situated just north of Thapsus in Roman Africa, the center area on the map. Utica can be made out near Carthage in the northernmost bay looking toward Sicily.

Roman Provinces of North Africa
Map of the Historical Atlas of Gustav Droysen, 1886

themselves by betraying the virtues he embodied. Someone then proposed giving the slaves their freedom, and most favored this proposal until Cato spoke against it. It was neither lawful nor just, he said, but he allowed that he would accept into the army any slaves of military age whom their masters freed. Many promised to do just that, and Cato ordered that their names be taken down and then took his leave of the assembly.

Not long after this, Cato received letters by messenger from Juba and Scipio. Juba was hiding with a few men in the mountains. He wanted to know Cato's plans, saying that he intended to wait for him if Cato decided to abandon Utica and otherwise would come to his aid if he was besieged. Scipio was lying at anchor off a headland not far from Utica also wanting to know Cato's intentions.

[61] Cato thought it best to have the messengers wait until he had learned what the Three Hundred would do. The men from the Senate were keen and had already freed their slaves and, once freed, had armed them. The Three Hundred, on the other hand, being merchants and bankers, whose property in large part consisted of **household slaves,** had lost much of their enthusiasm for Cato's words and were having second thoughts. As thin bodies are quickly heated when brought near the fire and soon cool once the fire is removed, just so Cato's rhetoric enflamed and heated these men, but when left to talk among themselves, their fear of Caesar cooled their ardor for Cato and his noble words. "Who are we, after all?" they reasoned, "and who is it we are planning to disobey? Is Caesar not the man on whom the entire power of Rome now rests? None of us is a Scipio, a Pompey, or a Cato. When fear has caused everyone we know to sell his honor cheap, why is it up to us to fight for the liberty of Rome? And why here in far-off Utica should we declare war against a man from whom Cato and Pompey the Great fled and to whom they abandoned Italy? Should we free our slaves to fight against Caesar, the man on whom our own future freedom depends? No, we must come to our senses and acknowledge how unimportant we are in the grand scale of things. Let us send envoys to the man with all the power and beg his mercy." At least this is how the more moderate members of the Three Hundred reasoned, but most of them wanted to seize the senators and hold them hostage, thinking that this might placate Caesar.

[61] **Household slaves**: the term would include, for these men of business, what we would call employees.

Cato Portion of an Allegorical Tapestry with Sages of the Past Unknown Artist. German, 1480–1500
The Met Collection.

[62] Cato suspected their change of heart but did nothing to persuade them otherwise. Instead, he sent the messengers off with letters to Juba and Scipio telling them to stay clear of Utica—the Three Hundred could not be trusted. Many of the cavalry that had escaped from the late battle now rode toward Utica and sent on ahead three men with widely differing opinions to meet with Cato. Some wanted to join up with Juba, others with Cato, and yet others were afraid to enter Utica. When Cato heard this, he ordered Marcus Rubrius to meet with the Three Hundred and quietly to take down the names of those who had freed their slaves of their own accord and without the use of force. Cato took the senators with him out of Utica to meet with the cavalry officers. He pleaded with the officers not to abandon so many Roman senators and not to choose Juba over Cato as their commander. He urged them to save the senators and themselves by coming into the city, arguing that its fortifications were impregnable and it possessed sufficient stores of grain and other provisions to last for years. The senators in tears made the same pleas. The officers then left to consult with their men while Cato and the senators sat down on a nearby embankment to await their response.

[63] At that moment, Rubrius came running up, angrily blaming the unpredictable Three Hundred for sowing revolt and disorder in the city. Hearing this the senators began to panic, bewailing and bemoaning their fate, while Cato tried to calm them down and sent word to the Three Hundred to wait for him. Meanwhile, the cavalry officers returned with impossible demands. They said they would not follow Juba for any price, nor would they fear Caesar so long as Cato led them. But they dreaded the thought of being shut up with the Uticans, in their opinion a bunch of fickle and treacherous Phoenicians. They might seem docile enough now, but as soon as Caesar appears, they will hatch a conspiracy and betray the Romans. "If you want us to join the fight with you," they demanded, "you must first kill or expel all the Uticans from the city, and in that way invite us into a city cleansed of all enemies and **barbarians**." Cato, aghast, listened to this proposal, considering it savage and **barbarous**, but he answered with complete composure that he would have to consult with the Three Hundred first.

Once back in the city, he found the men there no longer making excuses or out of respect for him pretending to tell him what they thought he wanted to hear. Instead, they said they would not be forced into making war against Caesar, and

[63] **Barbarians . . . barbarous**—In English, the cavalry officers undoubtedly would have called them "foreigners," which the Greek word can simply mean. But Plutarch then uses the same word with ironic effect to describe Cato's reaction, where the English "barbarous" is clearly wanted.

declared that they were neither willing nor able to do so. Some even went so far as to imply that the senators ought to be detained awaiting Caesar's arrival, but Cato pretended not to pick up on this last bit. Being slightly deaf, he had the perfect excuse. This exchange was interrupted when someone told Cato that the cavalry was about to leave. Now, fearing that in the absence of the cavalry, the Three Hundred might move against the senators, Cato pulled some of his friends aside and hastily excused himself. And seeing with his eyes the cavalry already riding off, he grabbed a horse and galloped after them. When they saw him coming, the cavalrymen were delighted and welcomed him to their ranks and invited him to save himself with them. It is reported that at this point Cato began shedding tears and pleading with arms outstretched in supplication on behalf of the endangered senators. By tugging at their mounts and pulling at their weapons, he eventually managed to get them turned around and willing to stay at least for one more day to provide a safe passage for the senators' flight.

[64] When he returned with the cavalry, he stationed some at the city gates and to others he gave charge of the citadel. The Three Hundred, now fearing that they would be punished for their about–face, sent a message to Cato urging him to come and see them. The senators, however, surrounded him and prevented him from going, saying they would not hand over their protector and savior to two–faced traitors.

It was at this time, perhaps more than at any other, when Cato's virtue shone forth most brightly because it was evident to everyone in Utica that in everything he did there was no element of trickery or deception or self–regard. Having decided to end his life, Cato resolved to suffer whatever pain and toil was necessary to ensure the safety of others before quitting this life. Even though he never spoke of it, it was clear he walked in the shadow of death.

After calming the senators down, he complied with the urgings of the Three Hundred and went to see them alone. They thanked him for all he had done for them and begged him still to use and trust them in the future. "Please take pity on our weakness," they pleaded. "We are just simple men and cannot all be Catos and aspire to your high–mindedness and greatness of soul." They told him that they had decided to send to Caesar and petition him for clemency, first and foremost for Cato, saying that if mercy were not granted to Cato, they would not accept it for themselves but

would fight on at his side as long as they drew breath. In answer, Cato praised them for their noble intentions and advised them, for the sake of their own safety, to make contact with Caesar as soon as possible. "But do not beg for mercy on my behalf," he said. "It is the defeated who beg for mercy and wrongdoers who ask forgiveness. In all my life, I have never known defeat and have always been victorious in those things that matter to me, besting Caesar in noble and just actions. Caesar is the one conquered and held captive. He is now caught in the act and convicted of doing against his country what he has so long dissembled and denied."

[65] Having said this, he left the Three Hundred only to learn that Caesar was already marching on Utica with his entire army. "How flattering!" Cato exclaimed, "Caesar is expecting to find men of courage here." Turning to the senators, he told them to make haste in saving themselves while the cavalry was still on hand. He ordered all the gates of the city shut except one leading to the sea, and to those who needed to leave the city, he assigned ships and provided them with provisions for the voyage ahead. He accomplished all of this in good order, settling disputes as they arose and putting down any disruptive behavior.

Marcus Octavius with two legions set up camp just outside the city. He sent to Cato asking him to resolve a conflict that had broken out concerning who should be in command. Cato didn't respond, but turning to his friends said, "How can we wonder why we have lost everything when even in the midst of ruin we are squabbling over who gets to be in charge?" Meanwhile, word was sent to him that **on their way out, the cavalry** was plundering the city and stealing the property of the Uticans. He ran after them and began stripping away the booty from the first horseman he encountered. Seeing this, the others—in shame and silence, staring all the time at the ground—threw down what they had taken as well.

After this, Cato called all the Uticans together and pleaded with them on behalf of the Three Hundred to stay together for their common safety and not to give Caesar reason to become vexed with them. Then he returned to the port to see off those who were embarking, embracing his friends and those he had persuaded to leave. He was not able to convince his son to save himself, however, and in the end he felt it somehow not right to ask a son to abandon his father.

There was a strong-willed and impulsive young fellow named Statyllius who wanted to follow the brave and unflappable example of Cato. Knowing how this

[65] **On their way out, the cavalry**: The cavalry's role in Plutarch's narrative, especially in the timing and content of this episode, presents the most striking contrast with the narrative we have in the *De Bello Africo*. The *Commentarii De Bello Africo*, or Report on the African War, is thought to have been written by one of Caesar's junior officers, a participant in events but not privy to the high command, a work described in the *Oxford Classical Dictionary* (1970) as "monotonous to the layman, but as military history it is painstaking and straightforward." As partisan as it obviously is, it is certainly no more partisan than Plutarch's source(s) and almost certainly far closer to the events. You will find in Appendix D a translation of the portion dealing with Utica, cc. 87–90. As you read, compare Plutarch's account, seeing where it seems to agree and why. Where the two accounts differ, try to account for the differences, deciding where the truth might lie and where gray areas remain.

lad made no secret of his hatred for Caesar, Cato asked him to set sail with the rest, but he refused. So Cato turned to Apollonides the Stoic and Demetrius the Peripatetic, saying, "It's up to you, my friends, to talk some sense into this earnest young man and make him see what's good for him." As for himself, he spent that night and most of the next day helping his friends embark and attending to many pressing demands.

[66] Lucius Caesar, a relative of Caesar's, now approached Cato and asked for his help in preparing a convincing speech to plead on behalf of the Three Hundred. "For your sake," he told Cato, "I would kiss Caesar's hands **and throw myself down at his knees**." But Cato would not hear of it. "If I had any wish to be saved by Caesar's favor," he said, "I would go to him alone, man to man. But I'm not about to thank a tyrant for breaking the law, and he breaks the law every time he grants mercy as lord and master over those he has no right to tyrannize. But let us consider instead, if you wish, what might be said to save the Three Hundred." Once they had decided on this, Cato entrusted the safety of his son and friends to Lucius and, taking him by the hand, bid him farewell.

Upon returning home, he called together his son and friends and spoke with them of many things and told his son not to become involved in politics. The situation no longer made it possible to act as he had done, and to act otherwise would be shameful. Now being evening, he took his bath. As he was washing, he suddenly remembered Statyllius and began calling out, "Apollonides! Did you succeed in talking sense to that young fellow and cooling his ardor? Has he gone off with the rest without saying goodbye?" "I'm afraid not," Apollonides responded, "we talked ourselves to death, but to no purpose. He remains resolute, determined to follow your example." To this, they say Cato commented, smiling, "Well, we'll soon see how his resolution stands the test."

[67] Having bathed, he joined a large company of friends and local magistrates for dinner, sitting rather than reclining, as was his custom. Since the debacle at Pharsalus, he only lay down to sleep. The drinks after dinner fueled a spirited and agreeable conversation that ranged over a number of philosophical topics until arriving at last at one of the so-called Stoic Paradoxes, the one stating that only

[66] `*And throw myself down at his knees*`: The classic action of an ancient suppliant, effective in that by embracing the knees you immobilize and force to respond the person from whom you are begging mercy.

good men are free, and bad men are all slaves. The **Peripatetic** inevitably began to object, but Cato cut him off and, in a rather heated and harsh tone, held forth at great length and with elaborate arguments defending the proposition, so much so that it became obvious to everyone that he had decided to free himself by ending his life. A mournful silence descended on the room. Cato, sensing the mood he had created, now tried to divert their suspicions and redirect the conversation by throwing out questions and concerns related to the present situation: what might become of those risking the perils of a long sea voyage, or of those fleeing by land through the parched and barren wilderness?

[68] After dinner, he went for a walk with his friends as was his habit. When they returned, he gave the officers of the guard their instructions for the night and retired to his rooms where he embraced his son and each of his friends with more than his usual warmth, causing them yet again to fear his intentions. Once in his bedchamber, he took up **Plato's dialogue concerning the soul**. He had almost finished the dialogue when he happened to glance above his head and notice that his sword was no longer hanging there. (His son had removed it while he was still at dinner.) He called his servant and asked who had taken his sword. When the servant said nothing, he went back to his reading. After waiting awhile so as not to seem in a hurry or upset, but still wanting his sword, he asked that it be brought to him. Time passed, but nobody came. He finished reading the dialogue and began to summon his servants, one at a time, and in a loud voice demanded his sword. He even struck one of them so hard on the mouth that he bloodied his hand and began shouting and complaining angrily that his son and servants were betraying him and handing him over naked to the enemy. This commotion brought his son and friends running. They entered his room in tears, falling to their knees and imploring him. But Cato stood up and looking sternly at them said, "Why are you treating me as if I'd lost my mind without realizing it? Why has no one attempted to reason with me or show me the error of my ways? Instead, you seek to deny me the use of both my reason and my sword. While you're at it, dear son, why not put your father in chains as well or tie his hands behind his back, so that Caesar will find him utterly powerless to defend himself? What, you think I need a sword to end this? All I need to do is hold my breath for awhile, or bang my head against that wall."

[67] **Peripatetic**: A follower of Aristotle's teaching would naturally object to this figurative use of the notion of slavery and freedom.

[68] **Plato's dialogue concerning the soul**: The *Phaedo* was known in antiquity as *On the Soul,* in which Socrates discusses the immortality of the soul with friends on the day before he is to drink hemlock. The dialogue ends with Phaedo's description of Socrates' death. It hardly seems likely that Cato could have read it through twice, as stated in [70], on the night before he died!

[69] As he said this, the boy left the room sobbing followed by all the others except Apollonides and Demetrius. To them he spoke more calmly, saying, "Are you also determined to keep a man of my age alive against his will? Or have you come here to spy on me? Or perhaps to persuade me that there is no shame or dishonor in bowing to fate and accepting from the hands of my enemy the only salvation now possible? Speak up! Reason with me. Persuade me that we were mistaken to live by the philosophy we were taught. Convince me that by learning from Caesar we might not only live longer but grow wiser. Fret not, I haven't yet made up my mind, but when I do, I want the power to act on my decision. Meanwhile, I'm counting on you to offer me sound advice and to counsel me in accordance with what our philosophy teaches us. And please tell my son that he should not try to force his father to do something he cannot persuade him to do."

[70] To this, they had nothing to say and left the room in tears. The sword was sent in with a small slave boy. Cato drew it from its sheath and inspected it, and seeing that the point was intact and the blade sharp, said, "At last I am my own master." Putting the sword aside, he picked up his book and read it through twice, they say. After this, he fell into such a deep sleep that those outside his chamber could hear him snoring. Around the middle of the night, he called for two of his freedmen, Cleanthes, his doctor, and Butas, to whom he usually assigned political tasks. He sent Butas to the port to make sure all of his friends had gotten off safely, and he asked the physician to bandage the hand that was swollen from the punch he had given his servant. These actions, interpreted as signs that he meant to go on living, raised everyone's spirits.

A little while later Butas returned to say that everyone except **Crassus** had gotten off, and that even Crassus, who had been delayed on business, was now about to embark. Butas also reported that it was blowing hard, and there appeared to be a great storm at sea. On hearing this, Cato sighed out of compassion for those who were at sea and sent Butas back to the port in case anyone should return and need his help.

He closed his eyes and dozed off again just as the birds began to sing. When Butas returned to tell him that all was calm at the port, he once again lay down

[70] **Crassus:** Publius Licinius Crassus Junianus was the pro–praetorian *legatus,* or second–in–command, to Scipio and now Cato.

on his bed as if to sleep through what remained of the night and asked Butas to close the door on his way out. But once Butas was gone, he took his sword and thrust it in below his chest. Because he was using his swollen hand, the thrust was weak, and he did not die immediately, but fell in agony from the bed knocking over a small bedside table on which he had been drawing geometric figures. Hearing this noise, the servants cried out, and his son and all his friends came running into the room where they found him drenched in blood with most of his entrails hanging out yet still alive and able to look at them. They gazed in horror. The doctor on the scene, seeing that the intestines were still intact, tried to push them back into the body and sew up the wound. But Cato, realizing what was happening, pushed the doctor away, tore open the wound, mangled his guts with his hands, and died.

[71] In less time than you would think it would take news of this to reach the members of the household, the Three Hundred were at the door, and not long after, the whole city of Utica came together. With one voice, they declared Cato **their benefactor, their savior, the only free, the only invincible man.** They made these declarations even as Caesar approached. Neither fear of the danger they were in, nor their desire to curry favor with the man in power, nor the factions that divided them and caused discord among themselves—none of this dulled the edge of their admiration and respect for Cato. They then lavishly prepared his body and organized a magnificent funeral before burying him by the sea at the spot where his statue now stands, sword in hand. Only after completing these rituals and tributes did they return to the city and consider how to save themselves.

[72] Upon learning from those who came to him that after sending the rest of the Romans away, Cato along with his son and friends remained in Utica, apparently unconcerned with their own safety, Caesar didn't know what to make of it. Nevertheless, perhaps out of profound respect, perhaps out of caution, he approached the city with his entire army. When at last he heard of Cato's death, he had only this to say, "O Cato, I begrudge you your death as you have begrudged me the opportunity to spare your life." The truth is, had Cato

[71] **Their benefactor, their savior, the only free, the only invincible man**: It has been reasonably conjectured that these epithets appeared in the inscription on Cato's tomb in Utica (*R.E.*: Porcius Cato).

allowed Caesar to spare his life it would not so much have diminished Cato's reputation as enhanced Caesar's. Would Caesar have spared Cato's life? We'll never know, of course, but we do know that he tended to lean toward clemency.

[73] Cato was forty–eight when he died. Cato's son was in no way mistreated by Caesar. But it is said that he grew lazy and became a promiscuous womanizer. In Cappadocia, he was the guest of Marphadates, a member of the royal family and husband of a very beautiful wife. He stayed with them much longer than he should have and became the target of literary jibes like these:

> *Tomorrow being the thirtieth day*
> *Cato may finally go away*

Or this one:

> *Porcius and Maphradates, two friends, one Psyche*
>   (Porcius another name for Cato, and Psyche the wife's name, which is
>   also the Greek word for Soul)

And this:

> *Noble and brilliant is Cato; indeed, he has a royal Soul.*

But his manner of dying completely blotted out the stain of all this gossipy scandal. While fighting for the liberty of Rome at **Philippi** against Caesar [Octavian] and Antony, and seeing that the line of battle was beginning to give way, he alone refused to yield, but stood his ground, calling out defiantly to the enemy and thereby rallying his troops. Although he fell in this battle, his enemies marveled at his death–defying bravery.

No less remarkable was Cato's daughter, whose disciplined living and brave dying were in no way inferior to her father's. She was married to Brutus, Caesar's assassin. She took part in the conspiracy against the tyrant and gave

[73] **Philippi**: After the assassination of Julius Caesar in 44 BC, the Battle of Philippi in 42 BC pitted Republican forces under Brutus and Cassius against the forces of Caesar's successors, Octavian and Mark Antony. It was the Republicans' "last stand" and very much a kind of epilogue to a Republic that had in fact ended, as the Republicans themselves saw it, with the death of Cato in Utica.

Death of Cato
Probably by Berardino Gentile, 1727–1813. Italian, hard red earthenware. The Met.

up her life in a manner worthy of her noble lineage and personal virtue. **All this I have described in my** *Life of Brutus*.

As for Statyllius, the headstrong young man who wanted to imitate Cato, he was only prevented from taking his own life by the philosophers. Later, he rendered very faithful and useful service to Brutus and was killed in battle at Philippi.

NOTES

All this I have described in my *Life of Brutus*: In his *Brutus* [53], following Brutus' loss and suicide at Philippi, Plutarch describes an account of her suicide. Deprived of other means by her watchful household, she dies by swallowing a burning coal.

181

APPENDICES

APPENDIX A
Excerpts from Isocrates' *To Philip* (346 BC on the occasion of the Peace of Philocrates)

[8] I rejoiced at the peace terms that were voted on and thought they would be beneficial not only to us but to you as well and to all the other Greeks. I could not help thinking about their consequences and immediately worked myself into a state thinking about how what had been achieved might endure for us, in order that our city might not allow a short time to pass before once again becoming eager for other wars. [9] Going over these things in my mind, I came to the conclusion that the only way for Athens to remain at peace was for the major city-states to decide to set aside their wars against each other and to carry their war into Asia, to decide, in other words, to satisfy their lust for more by taking from the barbarians what they now think best to take from each other.

[73] I sense that you are being misrepresented by those who are envious of you and who are in the habit of stirring up trouble in their own cities. They regard the peace shared by others to be a war against their own interests. Paying no attention to everybody else, they talk about your power as growing not on behalf of Greece but against her, saying that you have been plotting against us all for a long time. [75] By spouting this nonsense and pretending to be in the know, they quickly tear down everything with their words. And they convince many, especially those who invite the same disasters as the speakers. Then, there are those who do not give any thought to the commonweal but are completely insensitive in their way of thinking and are very grateful to men who pretend to be afraid on their behalf. Finally, there are those who do not deny that you are plotting against the Greeks but consider that your reason for doing so is worth it.

[127] For this reason, because the others are in this cowardly frame of mind, I believe it would be advantageous for you to lead the war against the King [of Persia]. *These others, descendants of Heracles, are bound by the laws in their constitutions and cling to the city-state in which they happen to live whereas you are not fenced in and are free to consider all of Greece as your homeland, as did your father. You may take risks on her behalf in the ventures that most inspire you.*

[128] There are perhaps some men, incapable of doing anything else, who will dare to criticize me for calling upon you to lead the expedition against the barbarians and to take care of the Greeks, leaving my own city [Athens] *aside. [129] If indeed I had undertaken to discuss these matters with any others before my own homeland that freed the Greeks thrice, twice from the barbarians and once from the rule of Sparta, I would confess my error. In fact, I am well known for having turned first to her with all the zeal of which I am capable, but when I realized that she thought less of what I said than she did of the ravings of speakers in the assembly, I let her be while never abandoning the business itself.*

APPENDIX B
Excerpts from Demosthenes' *Third Philippic* (341 BC)

[1] Men of Athens, many speeches have been delivered at nearly every meeting of the assembly concerning the wrongs committed by Philip since he made the peace [the Peace of Philocrates (346 BC)] *not only against you but against others also. And I know that all claim, even if they do not act accordingly, that something should be proposed and done to punish him and put an end to his arrogance. But I see that all our actions and plans have brought us to such a point—I fear it were blasphemous to utter but nonetheless true—that even if all those present were to propose and and to vote measures that would bring our affairs to the worst possible state, I don't believe they could be in any worse shape than they now are.*

[2] There are perhaps many reasons, not just one or two, that have brought us to this point. But if you look into it correctly you will find that it is especially owing to those who choose to say what is pleasing to hear rather than what is best for our city. Some of these, O men of Athens, in preserving a situation which gives them honor and authority, have no concern for the future and therefore think you shouldn't either; while others blame and slander those in authority and do nothing but seek to have the city punish its own while letting Philip do as he pleases.

[9] If there is anyone who understands "peace" to mean an arrangement by which Philip can take control of others before marching on us, he is surely mad. Or perhaps not mad but simply referring to the peace Philip gets from us and not the peace we get from him. This is what Philip buys with all the money he is spending, a way of making war on you without you making war on him.

[27] Are the cities in Euboea, an island close to Thebes and Athens, not already under the control of his tyrants? Does he not explicitly write in his letters: "I am at peace with those who wish to obey me"? He does not simply write such things; he acts on them. Now he is moving against the Hellespont; earlier he attacked Ambracia. The important city of Elis he now controls in the Peloponnese; the day before yesterday, he plotted against Megara. Neither in Greece nor abroad is there room for the man's greed.

[28] As Greeks, we see and hear about all this yet send no embassies to one another to complain. We are in such a sorry state and so entrenched in our own cities that, until this very day, we are able to accomplish nothing in our own interest, nothing that we ought. We are unable to unite, unable to create any community of assistance and alliance.

[29] We stand by watching the man grow greater, each of us taking advantage of the time he knows it will take for another to be destroyed, so it seems to me, instead of looking out and acting to save Greece. Meanwhile, Philip, like the recurrence or spread of a fever or some other disease, is approaching even the one who now thinks he is far off. Of this, no one is ignorant.

[63] Whatever is the reason, you may wonder, why those in Olynthus or Eretria or Oreus enjoyed listening to Philip's men more than to their own? It is the same with you. Because those who wish to say the truth are sometimes unable to say anything that pleases. They are obliged to look out for the city's safety. The others, by saying things that please, work in Philip's favor. [65] Better to die a thousand deaths than do anything to please Philip and betray your own!

APPENDIX C
Extract from Caesar's *Commentarii de Bello Gallico*, or *Report on the Gallic War*, Book IV, 13–15

[13] *Because of this battle* [the cavalry engagement], *Caesar decided that he would not listen to their ambassadors or honor conditions from men who, through treachery and traps, had asked for peace only to wage war. Indeed, he judged it to be the ultimate folly to wait for the enemy forces to increase and their cavalry to return. He also recognized the weakness of his Gallic forces sensing to what extent already a single battle had increased the enemy's reputation, and thought it best not to give them time to reconsider their loyalty. On these bases, he communicated his plan to his legates and quaestor not to put off the battle for a single day, when the most fortuitous thing happened: On the morning of the very next day, the Germans, with their usual perfidious pretense, came in great numbers to him in camp, all their leaders bringing with them their eldest sons, in order at one and the same time to absolve themselves for having joined battle the day before (as was said), contrary to what had been agreed and what they themselves had sought, and, if they could, to obtain a truce by means of deception. Delighted that they had offered themselves up to him, Caesar ordered them to be detained and, in person, led his troops out of camp, ordering the* [Gallic] *cavalry, which he believed had been terrified by the recent engagement, to follow in the rear.*

[14] *Forming a triple battle line and quickly completing the eight-mile march, he arrived at the enemy camp before the Germans could tell what was happening. They were suddenly terrified by everything, both the speed of our arrival and the disappearance of their leaders. Since they had no time to organize or arm, they were in a quandary whether it was better to attack, defend the camp, or seek safety in flight. Their terror was evident from the noisy tumult within, so our troops, aroused by the previous day's treachery, broke into the camp. There, those who were able to seize their weapons put up some resistance and joined battle amongst the supply wagons. The remaining multitude of women and children (for they had left their home and crossed the Rhine with all they had) began to scatter in flight. Caesar sent the cavalry to overtake them.*

[15] *When a shout was heard behind them, and they saw their men being killed, the Germans threw down their weapons and abandoned their standards and fled the camp.*

Once they had arrived at the confluence of the Meuse and the Rhine, no longer able to flee, a great number were killed, and the rest threw themselves into the river where, overwhelmed by fear, fatigue, and the current, they perished. Our men returned to camp having suffered no casualties and only a very few wounded after the fear of so great a war, when the enemy had numbered four hundred and thirty thousand strong. Caesar told the ones he had detained in camp they could leave. Dreading death by torture from the Gauls whose fields they had damaged, they said they wished to remain with him. Caesar granted them their freedom.

APPENDIX D
Extract from the *Commentarii De Bello Africo, or Report on the African War* [87]-[90]

[86] ... Marcus Messala went on ahead with the cavalry to Utica.

[87] Meanwhile, the men in Scipio's cavalry who had fled the battle and were making their way toward Utica arrived at the town of Parada [a town on Cape Bon across the bay from Utica] *where, since news of Caesar's victory had preceded them, they were not welcomed by the inhabitants. They took the town by force and inflicted on them the cruelest of punishments. Having built a great bonfire with branches and the people's belongings in the middle of the marketplace, they set it alight and threw in the inhabitants of both sexes and all ages, bound and still alive. They then made their way to Utica.*

Earlier, because Utica had benefitted from the Lex Iulia [Caesar's legislation], *Marcus Cato considered that there was too little protection for his partisans amongst the Uticans and had thrown the commoners unarmed outside of the town and forced them to live under guard in a camp outside the military gate he had fortified for this purpose with a small trench. The senators, however, he kept guarded in the town. When the cavalry came upon the camp, they attacked it and, knowing that the Uticans favored Caesar's partisans, they began avenging the pain of their loss by slaughtering them. The Uticans, however, their spirits lifted by Caesar's victory, drove the cavalry back with sticks and stones. So after they were unable to take the camp, the cavalry rushed into the town and there killed many Uticans, breaking into and plundering their homes. Since Cato was by no argument able to persuade the cavalry to join him in defending the town or to stop the killing and plundering, and since he knew what they wanted, for the sake of calming their insolence, he gave them a hundred sesterces each. Faustus Sulla* [the son of the former dictator by that name and son-in-law of Pompey] *did the same and, having also given them a gift of his own money, set out from Utica with them with the intention of reaching the kingdom* [i.e., of Juba in Numidia and Mauretania].

[88] Meanwhile, many people had fled to Utica. Cato called them all together along with the Three Hundred, who had provided funds for Scipio to pursue the war, and exhorted them to free their slaves to help defend the town. When he understood that some agreed, but some, terrified, had their heart and mind set on flight, he stopped pursuing this course and assigned them boats to sail each to his preferred destination. Once he had organized everything with the greatest diligence and entrusted his children to Lucius Caesar, who was his pro-quaestor at the time, and without arousing suspicion by looking and speaking as he had always done before retiring to sleep, he secretly carried a sword into his bedroom and pierced himself through. He collapsed before breathing his last, and the noise of his fall raised suspicions and brought a doctor and close friends into the bedroom. They immediately began to stop his guts from falling out and to sew up the wound. But with his own hands, he tore open the wound in the cruelest possible way and while fully conscious committed suicide. Although the Uticans had loathed him for political reasons, nonetheless, on account of his singular integrityand because he was most unlike the other leaders and had also fortified Utica with impressive walls and raised its towers, they built him a sepulcher. Once he was dead, Lucius Caesar, hoping to obtain some advantage from the situation, summoned the people to an assembly and called upon everyone to open the gates, saying that he had great hope in Caesar's clemency. And so, once all the gates were opened, he left Utica and set out to meet the commander Caesar. Messala, as he had been ordered, came to Utica and stationed guards at all the gates.

[89] [Caesar's movement from Thapsus to Hadrumentum is described to the point when he continues his movement toward Utica and meets Lucius Caesar.] *When Lucius Caesar met him on the road, he threw himself to his knees and begged only that his life be spared. This, Caesar easily granted, both because it was in his nature and because it was his policy. As was his habit, he bestowed the same on Caecina, Caius Ateius, Publius Atrius, Lucius Cella, father and son, M. Eppius, M. Aquinus, Cato's son, and to the children of Damasippus. With torches lit all around, he arrived at Utica and spent the night outside the town.*

[90] Early on the following morning, he entered the town and called an assembly. He encouraged the residents of Utica and thanked them for their zeal on his behalf. The Roman citizens and businessmen and those from among the Three Hundred who

had contributed funds to Varus and Scipio, however, he accused at length. At the very end of a rather long speech detailing their crimes, he announced that they could show their face without fear. He would go so far as to grant them their lives. Their property he would sell, but in such a way that, should someone wish to buy back his own property, Caesar would extend the sale so that by paying a fine the owner could keep it without hindrance. Pale with fear and rightly despairing for their lives, they gladly and greedily jumped at his offer once their safety had been offered them and asked Caesar to demand a single amount to be paid by the Three Hundred as a body. Caesar therefore fixed a sum of two hundred thousand sesterces to be paid to the Roman people in six installments over a period of three years. No one balked at this. They thanked Caesar, proclaiming that on this day they were born again.

BIBLIOGRAPHY

GREEK TEXTS

Flacelière et Chambry. *Plutarque Vies.* Tome x. Paris: Les Belles Lettres, 2003.

Ziegler, Konrat. *Plutarchi Vitae parallelae.* Vol. II, fasc. 1. Leipzig: Teubner, 1964. (Bibliotheca Teubneriana).

Secondary works cited

Addison, Joseph. *Cato: A Tragedy and Other Selected Essays.* Indianapolis: Liberty Fund, 2004.

Braudel, Fernand. *Le Méditerranée et le monde méditerranéen à l'époque de Philippe II.* Paris: Armand Colin Editeur, 1966, 1990.

Chroust, Anton-Hermann and John R. Murphy. *Lex Acilia and the Rise of Trial by Jury in the Roman World*, 24 Notre Dame: L. Rev. 1, 1948.

Cambridge Ancient History. Cambridge: CUP, 1951.

Fowke, Ph. and Waller, Stephen. *Plutarch's Lives.* New York and London: Harper & Brothers.

Hammond, N., *A History of Greece to 323 BC*, Oxford: OUP, 1959.

Aurelius, Marcus. *The Emperor's Handbook*. Translated by C. Scot Hicks and David V. Hicks. New York: Scribner, 2002.

Plutarch, *The Lawgivers*. Translated by C. Scot Hicks and David V. Hicks. Concord, NC: CiRCE Institute, 2019.

Quinn, Kenneth, *Catullus, The Poems, edited with introduction, revised text and commentary.* Macmillan Education: London, 1973.

de Romilly, Jacqueline, *La douceur dans la pensée grecque.* Paris: Les Belles Lettres, (1979).

Plato, *The Republic*. Translated by Richard W, Sterling and William C. Scott. Norton, 1985.

Syme, Ronald, *The Roman Revolution*. Oxford: OUP 1960.

Wills, Garry, *Cincinnatus, George Washington and the Enlightenment.* Doubleday, 1984.